Ab

Ed and I... sort of. ;-)

Michael Kohler lives in northern California. He has a Master's Degree in Education, a Bachelors Degree in Liberal Studies from Chico State University, and a degree in Business Administration from Feather River College.

Michael can be contacted at: michael@coralcastleexplained.com

Thank You

I would like to thank the many people that helped me make this ebook possible. I would like to thank my family and friends for their support and help. You know who you are.

I would like to thank the people at the Coral Castle for their excellent information and help.

Most of all, I would like to thank Ed Leedskalnin for his amazing achievement which inspired me to write this book to share with the world.

Dedication

To my father Merlin Kohler 1928-2006

This book is dedicated to my father, Merlin Kohler, for his love, understanding, and support of a son that always had his head in the clouds, and who, perhaps, has created something of value that his father can be proud of...

You can see the comet he discovered, Comet Kohler, by going here:

http://www.CometKohler.com

Table Of Contents

Chapter 1 – Two Castles – Two Histories
Chapter 2 – A Brief History of the Coral Castle – Standard Version
Chapter 3 - A Brief History of the Coral Castle – Enhanced Version
Chapter 4 – A Riddle in Stone
Chapter 5 – The "First Coral Castle" or "Ed's Place"
Chapter 6 – Symbolism and Architecture at "Ed's Place"
Chapter 7 – The "Second Coral Castle" or "Rock Gate Park"
Chapter 8 – Symbolism and Architecture at "Rock Gate Park"
Chapter 9 – Signs of "Sweet Sixteen"
Chapter 10 – The Monkey in the Shells
Chapter 11 – Phi in the Stones
Chapter 12 – A Glitch in the Theory?
Chapter 13 – Hyperdimensional Physics and Phi
Chapter 14 – It's in the Geometry, Stupid!
Chapter 15 – Water and Earth Energy
Chapter 16 – Frequencies and Water
Chapter 17 – The Giza Coral Castle Connection
Chapter 18 – Calcite and the Pineal Gland
Chapter 19 – Morphogenetic Fields and Intent
Chapter 20 – How Ed "Got the Power"
Chapter 21 – A Journey of Discovery
Chapter 22 – An Unexpected Encounter
Chapter 23 – Measurement of a Ghost
Chapter 24 – Ed's Last Words
Chapter 25 – Why Ed Died
Chapter 26 – Merkabah and Hemispheric Synchronization

Chapter 27 – How We Can Do What Ed Did
Chapter 28 – Why the Coral Castle is Important
Conclusion
Chronology of Edward Leedskalnin
Sources
Resource Links

Introduction
What is the Coral Castle?

The Tower at the Coral Castle

Throughout the ages, unique and interesting cultures all over the world have created amazing structures that have intrigued the minds of many worldwide. From Machu Picchu in Peru, to the great pyramids in Egypt, these massive megalithic structures have always posed this question:

How did the ancient cultures move these incredibly large stones with such precision using only primitive tools? It is not only the sheer size of the stones, but the techniques that the ancients used to cut, move, and position the stones with laser precision.

Skeptics and main stream scientists have claimed that the use of primitive tools with a lot of time and manpower is probably the solution to how the ancient builders created their magnificent structures.

However, one man stands apart from all of the ancient stone builders, displacing the commonly held beliefs that primitive tools, lots of manpower, and a lots of time, is needed to build a megalithic structure.

His name is Edward Leedskalnin.

Less than 100 years ago, in South Florida, a 5 foot tall, 100 pound man of Latvian descent, created an 1100 ton structure built out of solid coral.

He not only built the structure once, but actually disassembled the original, moved it, and reassembled it with no help from modern equipment or his fellow man.

Ed's creation, the Coral Castle, is a testament to anyone that doubts that the ancient stone builders utilized a powerful, but forgotten natural technology, that enabled them to cut, move, and position stones of enormous weight and size without the use of ropes, pulleys, cranes, hydraulics, or even laser precision tools.

Thought lost for over 50 years, his secret has finally been rediscovered. Edward Leedskalnin did not die with his secrets still in him.

Ed left them in plain sight for all of us to see, encoded in the symbolism, mathematics, geometry, and astronomical alignments of the Coral Castle itself.

Ed said he knew the secrets of the builders of the pyramids, and now you will too, as you read the inner secrets of "The Coral Castle Explained."

Chapter 1
Two Histories - Two Castles

Entrance to the Coral Castle

As the historic novel by Charles Dickens, "A Tale of Two Cities" says, "It was the best of times, it was the worst of times".

This phrase, possibly one of the most famous lines in all of English literature, is a good summary of the life of Ed Leedskalnin.

From the low of being jilted at the altar by his "Sweet Sixteen", to the high of creating one of the most amazing stone structures in the world, Ed's life has always been associated with 2 things:

The Coral Castle Coral Castle that he built. The secrets that died with him. I believe that I have rediscovered how Ed Leedskalnin was able to move and manipulate 1100 tons of coral, and it was not with the use of primitive tools.

To explain Ed's secret to you, I must start with a brief history of Ed himself. There are, in fact, two histories, one which I call the

"Standard Version" and the one that I call the "Enhanced Version."

Please read them in order as you will clearly see that the standard history leaves out some very important aspects and clues that lead us toward solving this "riddle in stone."

Pay close attention to these 3 key points:

1. The dates that each "Coral Castle" was built (yes, there were two versions)
2. Ed's age as each one is built
3. The chronology of events in Ed's life

All of these aspects play a crucial role in understanding the overall motivations of Ed, and the secret that he discovered which allowed him to create a structure that has no rival in contemporary times.

By the end of this book, you will understand how unique and important this amazing structure is.

At the very least, you will have a complete understanding of how the Coral Castle was built, why it was built, and what it means to us today.

With that said, let's jump right in and learn about the Coral Castle, and how one man, Edward Leedskalnin, an immigrant from Latvia, decided that it was "a far, far better thing" to build a monument of love to his "Sweet Sixteen" that ended up becoming the greatest "riddle in stone" ever created.

Chapter 2
A Brief History of the Coral Castle Standard Version

Author at the Coral Castle sign

This brief history that I call the "Standard Version" is a compilation of the information that I have found on websites, heard from guests on radio shows, and have read personally in the sanctioned books that are sold at the Coral Castle gift shop itself.

It is generally accepted that Edward Leedskalnin, who liked to be called Ed, was born in the year 1887 in the country of Latvia. At the age of 26, Ed was engaged to marry the girl of his dreams, Agnes Scuffs, who was 16 years old. On the day before the wedding, she told Ed that she did not want to marry him for one of many reasons.

It has been said that he was too old, too poor, or perhaps did not have enough education (Ed was said to have only had a fourth-grade education).

Due to his dreams being shattered by his "Sweet Sixteen," Ed left

Latvia, traveled to Canada, and then subsequently down into California and Texas. During this time, Ed is said to have worked in the lumber industry and was part of at least one cattle drive in Texas.

These jobs were said to have given him the strength necessary to move the enormous blocks of coral that he would later use in making the Coral Castle.

During his travels, Ed developed a case of tuberculosis. He then traveled from Texas to Florida in search of a better climate to help him with his newly developed disease.

Ed arrived in Florida and began building the Coral Castle on land that he purchased for $12.

After curing himself of tuberculosis, Ed spent the next 20 to 30 years building this monument made of coral in dedication to his "Sweet Sixteen".

At some point, Ed decided to move the Coral Castle for one of many reasons:

1. a new subdivision building nearby that was impinging upon his privacy
2. a brutal beating by thugs looking for money, motivating him to move for his personal safety
3. a miscalculation regarding the supernatural energies that he may have used to carve and move these great coral pieces.

Whatever the reason was, Ed relocated his coral home of stone to Homestead, Florida, roughly 10 miles north of his Florida City location, and renamed it "Rock Gate Park" after the 9-ton gate he installed after moving to this new location.

Ed made his living by giving tours of the Coral Castle and

published several pamphlets on astronomical and electromagnetic information, as well as created what appears to be a perpetual energy device, before his death.

Ed died at the age of 64 of stomach cancer in December of 1951 at Jackson Memorial Hospital in Miami.

Unfortunately, it seems that all of the secrets that Ed possessed, including his ability to carve and move megalithic stones, and the secrets of his perpetual energy device, died with him over 50 years ago.

Yet, because of the Coral Castle, and his writings, the mystery of Edward Leedskalnin lives on today.

What you have just read is a typical explanation of the life and times of Edward Leedskalnin, the creator of the Coral Castle.

In the next chapter, in what I call the "Enhanced Version" of the history of Edward Leedskalnin, there are many more details that set the foundation for understanding the mystery of Ed and his Coral Castle.

You will learn that Ed's secret was never "lost" at all, and that it has, in fact, been staring us in the face for over 50 years.

Chapter 3
A Brief History of the Coral Castle Enhanced Version

Entrance to the Coral Castle

What you will notice in this version of the "history of Ed" is the addition of dates, Ed's age, and a chronology of events that, when placed in order, give us not only an idea of Ed's motivations, but give us more insight into the mystery of Ed and the Coral Castle itself.

As stated in the previous chapter, It is generally accepted that Ed was born in 1887. At the age of 26, he was going to marry his "Sweet Sixteen" Agnes Scuffs. Therefore, Ed was 26 years old in the year 1913.

After being jilted at the altar by Agnes, Ed leaves Latvia heartbroken, travels to Canada, California, Texas, and then finally ends up in Florida with an advanced case of tuberculosis.

What is interesting is that despite the humid climate of South

Florida, which would have theoretically been bad for his tuberculosis, he apparently traveled there from Texas and ended up in Florida City seeking a better climate for his illness.

According to the literature, this occurred between the years of 1918 and 1920. Ed, at this time, would have been between 31 and 33 years of age. According to Joe Bullard, author of the book "Waiting for Agnes", Ed was found on the side of the road in Florida City by a real estate man named Moser.

Moser and his wife allowed Ed to stay on their back porch even though he had tuberculosis. Due to their kindness, Ed was able to somehow conquer tuberculosis and then purchased a piece of property two miles south of Florida City and began construction of the "First Coral Castle" dedicated to his "Sweet Sixteen".

This first version of the Coral Castle was not like the one that is currently at Homestead Florida. It was more like a garden of very large rocks, all of which were later moved to the Homestead site.

Ed earned his money by giving tours of his rock garden at the tune of $.10 a visitor. The particular coral that Ed used is a very non-porous oolite coral that has a very layered or sedimentary appearance to it.

As it says in the pamphlets that you receive at the Coral Castle, this particular coral and the items that Ed carved, have a very smooth and almost natural appearance to them. Not of carved pieces chiseled out with primitive tools, but it seems as if they were "naturally grown."

Most of the coral pieces at the Florida City site, with the exception of some of the larger ones, seem to resemble furniture and seem to also reflect Ed's desire to have his "Sweet Sixteen" come back to him so that they could raise a family in this "home" that Ed had created out of stone.

According to Ed's booklet "A Book in Every Home," the total weight of all of the pieces that were carved at the site was about 200 tons. Ed lived at this location until 1937.

According to Orval Irwin, who was a close friend of Ed's and author of "Mr. Can't Is Dead," Ed decided to move from his Florida City location to a new location located in Homestead Florida.

According to Orval, Ed had purchased 10 acres of land at Homestead and wanted to move not because a new subdivision was building nearby, or that he was beaten up and fearing for his life. Ed decided to move because "he felt isolated at his current location."

This makes sense since Ed bought his property directly adjacent to Highway 1, the main route of traffic between Miami and the Keys.

By the way, Ed at this time was 50 years old. Contracting with the young Orval Irwin for his moving services, Orval and Ed first moved all of Ed's "primitive tools" to the Homestead location and locked them securely away in a coral pit that Ed had dug out and secured with a ladder and chain.

There was nothing else on this barren 10 acres of land. Afterwards, Ed then hired another man by the name of Bob Biggers and began to move his megalithic coral creations, one of which weighed 30 tons, using Bob Biggers tractor and his solid rubber tire trailer up Highway 1.

This caused the local news media, specifically the Redland District News, to do an article about Ed's "colossal move" in July of 1939. This was also the year that Ed completed his move, and resurrected the original 200 tons of coral at the Homestead site.

This was also the year that Ed began a new major addition to what we now call the Coral Castle. Ed was now 52 years old.

The new editions that Ed added included the wall that surrounds the Coral Castle complex, the Polaris telescope, and a variety of other coral objects using the native coral (also oolitic limestone) on his 10 acres of land. Ed cut, moved, and placed all of the new coral blocks between the years 1939 and the end of 1940, or basically in less than two years.

According to Ed's booklet "A Book In Every Home" and the Coral Castle pamphlets, the total weight of all the new editions that he added at the Homestead location was 900 tons of coral. That is 900 tons of coral, cut, moved, and positioned, in less than 2 years by Ed Leedskalnin, with primitive tools, working alone.

Ed was now almost 54 years old.

According to Orval Irwin, in 1940, Ed opened for business again because the entire Coral Castle structure, all 1100 tons of it, was in place and ready for public viewing.

This time he may have charged up to 25 cents a tour instead of the original 10 cents (although his original money collecting stone is still displayed outside the Coral Castle stating that admission is only 10 cents).

Between 1940 and 1945, Ed began to make astronomical observations, published several pamphlets on electromagnetism and created what some believe to be a perpetual motion energy generator, despite his rumored 4th grade education.

The remnants of this free energy device are still in the "tool room," which is directly below Ed's living quarters of the 243 ton "Tower" that he lived in until his death.

The ending of this "Enhanced Version" of the history of Ed Leedskalnin ends the same as before.

In December of 1951, at the age of 64, Ed Leedskalnin died at Jackson Memorial Hospital in Miami of stomach cancer.

Now that you have read both the "Standard" and "Enhanced" versions of Ed's history, the next chapter contains a few points for you to consider, leading us toward understanding Ed's "riddle in stone" called the Coral Castle.

Chapter 4 - A Riddle in Stone

Entrance to the "Tower" where Ed lived

You will notice that the "Enhanced Version" of the Ed's journey from Latvia to Homestead includes a lot of information that is typically left out of most accounts of Ed Leedskalnin.

It is not that this information is not available, or there is some conspiracy to keep it out of the public eye. I have just taken information that is available, and put it in a chronological order.

The reason that I have stated the years of each move and Ed's age at the time, is to paint a different picture than is commonly accepted about Ed, and to address a variety of explanations about how and why he created and moved the Coral Castle.

For instance, I was always under the impression that Ed was a much younger man when he first began construction of the Coral Castle. Ed was between the age of 31 and 33 when he had his tuberculosis.

Therefore, even if he was a strong man, he had just recovered from tuberculosis before starting his work on carving and moving these enormous blocks of coral. I was also under the impression that Ed was a recluse and lived at the Coral Castle because he was a hermit.

However, when you read Orval Irwin's book "Mr. Can't Is Dead," you realize that Ed was a very sociable person that invited people over from the local church to roast hot dogs, liked to attend movies, and was often seen in public.

The most telling statement of Ed's need to attract more people into his life, if not more money, was his desire to move his existing coral structure to a new location in Homestead Florida because he felt isolated.

Moreover, the new location that Ed purchased in Homestead Florida was 10 acres directly on the side of Highway 1 (also called the [Dixie Highway](#) as noted on the Coral Castle's [physical address](#)) which is the main route of traffic between Miami and the Florida Keys.

If Ed was such a recluse, and did not like people, or was worried about a subdivision impinging on his privacy, why would he have chosen to move his place of residence directly next to the busiest street in southern Florida?

When Ed moved from Florida City to Homestead, he was 50 years old. Not that 50 years of age is old, but he was not a spring chicken either.

Prior to moving the 200 tons of existing coral, Orval Irwin and Ed moved all of his "primitive tools" before he hired Bob Biggers.

This means, at the very least, that Ed loaded Bob Biggers' solid rubber tire flatbed without the use of his "primitive tools", opening the possibility that Ed was using some other technique for moving these enormous stones.

And finally, after Ed had finished moving all of his stones from Florida City, and had set them up, he started adding on to what we now call the Coral Castle. The total weight of all of the stones at Coral Castle is estimated to be 1100 tons.

Therefore, if Ed moved 200 tons of coral initially, and then added on, this means that Ed cut, moved, and positioned 900 tons of coral in less than two years!

This is quite a feat for a 5 foot tall, 100 pound man with primitive hand tools. Even more interesting, while doing this, on the side of Highway 1, the busiest highway in south Florida, no one, including Bob Biggers, ever saw him move one single solitary piece of coral. How is this possible?

There are some reports of witnesses that purportedly saw Ed working, one of which said that Ed was singing to the stones while they floated like hydrogen balloons in the air. Orval Irwin, author of "Mr. Can't Is Dead" said that Bob Biggers never saw Ed unload because Ed would always ask him to leave before he loaded or unloaded the solid rubber tire trailer.

Regardless of the reasons why no one ever saw Ed move a single piece of coral, the fact is that the 1100 ton Coral Castle stands today, not because of primitive tools, but due to an ancient secret that Ed rediscovered.

The next couple of chapters will take a look at each stage of Ed's Coral Castle. I will look at both versions, examining the symbology and architectural change of each stage of the structure that finally became the Coral Castle.

The reason for examining each stage of construction at each site is that this will provide clues as to how Ed was able to cut and move these enormous stones, and reveals his ultimate purpose in creating the Coral Castle that we all know today.

The Coral Castle, in my opinion, is a giant 1100 ton puzzle in stone, reflecting the mind of Ed Leedskalnin. He left this megalithic structure, not only as his legacy, but a riddle in stone that hides the secrets of anti gravity, free energy, and intent. I believe I have deciphered this riddle. Let's begin with Florida City...

Chapter 5
The First Coral Castle or "Ed's Place"

Cardboard replica of Ed in his room

The "First Coral Castle" to my knowledge had no name. Orval Irwin referred to it as "Ed's place." So whether I call it the "First Coral Castle" or the "Florida City site" or "Ed's rock garden," either way, I am referencing the same thing: Ed's first version of what is now called the Coral Castle.

After conquering tuberculosis, Ed purchased 1 acre of land for $12 in the Florida City area. This place was more or less a garden of rocks, most of which were carved in a way that represented the interior of a home.

All of Ed's creations in this rock garden were made of the native Oolite coral in the area. There were many tables and chairs. There was an area for children to play. There was a so-called "Throne Room" with various chairs including the mother-in-law chair, the most uncomfortable chair in Ed's collection based upon its very straight back.

Ed had also created a bathtub, several beds, a cradle for a baby, a circular sombrero shaped chair, what is known as the "Sun Couch", and various other coral items.

The largest and heaviest of Ed's creations were the "Moon Fountain" (a 23 ton circular coral pond with two 18 ton crescent moon shaped chairs), the "Crescent of the East" (a 23 ton 20 foot tall piece of coral that resembles a crescent moon), and "The Great Obelisk" (which is a single piece of coral that stands 40 feet high and weighs over 28 tons).

The Coral Castle pamphlets mention that the Obelisk, as it stands now at the Coral Castle in Homestead, is in a 6 foot deep hole carved to perfectly fit this enormous coral piece.

I am going to assume that the Obelisk was in a similar hole at the Florida City site, not only for support, but because of what its purpose was in regard to how Ed carved and moved the coral blocks. (More on this later)

To conclude, these three larger pieces, along with all of the "furniture" that Ed carved and maneuvered weighed in excess of 200 tons.

What is even more interesting than the staggering weight of these coral pieces is the symbolism represented by the larger pieces.

In the next chapter, we will look at the re-occurring symbolism which gives us clues toward how Ed originally carved and moved these enormous pieces of coral.

Chapter 6
The Symbolism and Architecture at "Ed's Place"

28 Ton 40 foot high oolite "Obelisk"

To understand how Ed may have created and maneuvered these enormous chunks of coral, we must look at the symbolism and architecture that was created at the original site at Florida City.

This is important because the symbolism and architecture at the Homestead site is completely different than that used at Florida City. This difference in symbolism and design illustrates an important evolution in the mind of Ed Leedskalnin.

Ed seems to have begun with an original system for creating and moving the coral, and ends up taking what I call "a path of discovery" that is apparent as you go from one site to the next.

At "Ed's Place" or the "First Coral Castle" at Florida City, there are three symbolic representations and a common theme that are replicated at the second Coral Castle site.

The three symbols that we want to focus upon are:

1 - the 6 pointed star
2 - the moon and its phases
3 - the number 16

The re-occurring common theme that we want to focus upon is: water

Let's look at these symbols:

Symbol # 1 - The 6 pointed star

The 6 pointed star is seen in several places in the coral that came from the Florida City site. It is seen:

1 - At the top of the "The Great Obelisk"
2 - Above Ed's bathtub, inscribed in the coral wall
3 - In the middle of the 23 ton Moon Fountain
4 - The shape of the small table in the area for children that Ed called "Grotto of the Three Bears" 5 - On top of the miniature tower that Ed used to collect 10 cents for his tours
6 - A small chair that sits near the end of the North Wall

Symbol #2 - The Moon

The moon and its phases are represented by:

"The Crecent of the East"
"The Moon Fountain" and accompanying crescent moon chairs.

Symbol #3 - The Number 16

The number 16 can be found:

16 symmetrically placed bevels placed on the inside the lip of the 23 ton fountain
16 stairs leading to the top of the Tower
16 rays of light extending from the Sun on the drawing etched on a metal door

Reoccurring theme - Water

Water can be found associated with most occurrences of the 6 pointed star, the moon and the number 16.

So what does the symbolism mean and how does it all connect together? And how does this symbolism connect with water?

Before I answer these questions, let me make one more statement about the 6 pointed star.

There have been many people that have stated that the 6 pointed star represents the Latvian star, which I have seen on the Internet.

However, Orval Irwin, Ed's close friend, documents that a visitor once asked Ed if he was Jewish. Ed replied that he was not Jewish and that the 6 pointed star was simply a geometric pattern that is found in nature.

This is very important. If you connect the dots of the 6 pointed star, you also get another shape that is found in nature: a hexagon. We will come back to this later.

To conclude, Ed's original architecture that he developed at the Florida City site, seems to be focused upon nature.

The moon, its phases, water, and the 6 pointed star, are naturally occurring objects, effects, substances, and shapes that are found in nature, all of which, as you will see, are directly related to the number 16.

Later, you will see what these symbols mean and how they were utilized by Ed to move, cut, and position the coral pieces at both locations.

You will also understand how the number 16 connects everything together. Now let's take a look at the "Second Coral Castle" or "Rock Gate Park," the current and final version of the Coral Castle that is located in Homestead, Florida.

Chapter 7
The Second Coral Castle or "Rock Gate Park"

Interior shot of the Coral Castle courtyard

Ed lived at his Florida City residence from around 1918 or 1920 until 1937. In 1937, at the age of 50, Ed decided that he wanted to move. As I have already stated, there have been many theories as to why Ed moved.

Some believe that a new subdivision was moving in nearby and that Ed felt that his privacy was going to be inundated. Others say that he was attacked and beaten and had decided to move for personal safety.

Another theory states that Ed felt that the natural energy or leyline that helped him move his coral blocks had shifted and that he needed to move 10 miles north to Homestead in order to ensure that this energy would still be available.

Although all of these theories are plausible, I have a different opinion as to his motivation for moving.

As I mentioned in Chapter 4, Orval Irwin states a couple of things in his book "Mr. Can't Is Dead" that seem to paint a different picture of Ed's motivations.

In 1936, Ed had printed his very first book "A Book In Every Home" which basically offers his thoughts on Agnes, as well as his domestic and political viewpoints.

In 1937, Ed told Orval Irwin that he wanted to move because he felt too isolated at his Florida City location. In reality, Ed made his living by offering tours of his coral residence.

Therefore, his decision to move to his new location in Homestead, directly on the side of Highway 1, clearly shows me that Ed was moving, not to get more privacy or hide from would-be attackers, but that he moved in order to attract more visitors.

Ed was obviously a businessman. He offered his pamphlets for sale in newspapers. He charged for his tours. In fact, Ed was very much like a magician. He had a show to sell and would never reveal the secret to his tricks, with his tricks being his ability to maneuver and carve massive coral blocks of stone.

Another clue that Orval Irwin gives us in his book is this: He had asked Ed why he never mentioned his "Sweet Sixteen" anymore once he had moved and fully set up his Coral Castle in Homestead.

Ed's reply was, "Oh, I left her down at Florida City and don't talk about her anymore."

It could be assumed that Ed finally realized that Agnes was never going to show up after 20 years. Perhaps he realized that his home of coral, that he created for his potential family, would never be used for anything more than a sideshow attraction to earn him money.

Therefore, you could also assume that Ed wrote his book "A Book In Every Home" in 1936 to finally express how he felt about his "Sweet Sixteen." With his feelings publicly exposed, he was able to move on and create something new.

Something unbelievably large and new.

Therefore, it is my belief that Ed may have created the "First Coral Castle" or "Ed's Place" for his "Sweet Sixteen" when he still believed that she might one day come to him.

However, at the age of 50, he came to the realization that she was never going to show up. He may have also realized that his "real family" were the people that came and actually visited him and allowed him to give the tours of his coral creations that seemed to make him so happy.

I personally believe that "Sweet Sixteen" was much more than a person that caused grief in Ed's life, motivating him to create this amazing structure. I believe that "Sweet Sixteen" was also a code for the secret to how Ed accessed the energy that allowed him to move 1100 tons of coral.

As I have already mentioned in my brief history of Ed Leedskalnin, the rock garden at Florida City, the "First Coral Castle", consisted of 200 tons of coral made of a nonporous coral with a layered appearance.

After moving this coral between 1937 and 1939, Ed began a massive addition to his existing coral adding an additional 900 tons of coral blocks and structures in a period of less than two years.

In the next chapter, I will discuss the symbolism and architecture of this second and final version of the Coral Castle, and show you how it relates to mathematics, geometry and science.

Chapter 8
The Symbolism and Architecture at "Rock Gate Park"

"Throne Room" at the Coral Castle

One of the most obvious differences between the coral that comes from Florida City and the coral that was harvested and used at the Homestead site is that the Florida City coral pieces are generally smooth and without distinct edges.

The chairs seemed to be molded. The beds and cradle and even the larger pieces like the "Moon Fountain" and "The Crescent of the East" are made of a darker, layered, much smoother composition than the coral that is indigenous to the Homestead site.

The 900 tons of coral that Ed added directly out of the ground at the Homestead site is a porous, lighter colored coral, similar to that which you would see while snorkeling in the water.

The coral pieces are cut in a very blocky, rectilinear format. In essence, it seems as if Ed changed his style from that of a sculptor to someone playing with enormous Lego blocks. Here is a quick rundown on some of his creations at the Homestead site.

Ed created a stone wall that nearly surrounds this entire new complex, consisting of 420 tons of rectangular blocks of coral that weigh on the average 6 1/2 tons each. These blocks were taken directly out of quarries that surrounded his work area, one of which is still visible today.

The wall itself surrounds most of the Florida City coral creations in a square format (though depicted as rectangular on the brochures).

This is important to note, because it plays a large role regarding how I discovered the secret to "Sweet Sixteen."

Next, Ed created a two story tower at the southwest corner that would serve as both his tool room and his upstairs residence. This was made of 243 tons of coral using rectangular blocks, some weighing as much as 9 tons each.

Ed also created what is called the "Polaris Telescope". This tall rectangular 28 ton structure is perfectly aligned with the North Star Polaris.

(Note: The Polaris Telescope is one of the largest pieces of coral that Ed carved and erected at the Homestead site. For people that doubt that Ed added the 900 tons of coral in just 2 years, this 28 ton, 25 foot tall piece of coral has the date of its completion inscribed on it: 1940.

If the blocks that make up the walls of the Coral Castle were only 6.5 tons each, by comparison, it should have been "easy" for Ed to get them into place first, allowing him to finish working on everything else without being seen by passersby. This makes sense since the only images of Ed "working" were taken by Ed himself using a Brownie Box camera with a timer according to the excellent work of Rusty McClure in his Coral Castle book.)

Looking through a triangular piece of coral that has a hole with wire crosshairs, you can see the North Star at night through the hole and crosshairs at the top of this magnificent structure.
The ability to properly line up a 28 ton piece of coral with Polaris is an amazing engineering feat all by itself, regardless of the size and weight of the object that was moved and erected.

He also seems to have aligned the complex with the cardinal points, something that ancient megalithic structures like the Great Pyramid of Giza are also aligned with. He also created a sundial that measures the astronomical orbit of the Earth around the sun.

If you have not already noticed, the point I am trying to make is that Ed has completely deviated from creating anything that does not have a linear or blocky format. Ed's old focus on symbology, the moon, the phases of the moon, the 6 pointed star and water have shifted to a new focus: mathematics, geometry, and science.

There is one constant, however, that Ed has carried over from the Florida City site to the Homestead site: it is the number 16.

In the next chapter, I will begin to show you how the number 16 relates to both sites and how it is the secret to how Ed was able to access the energy necessary to quarry and move 1100 tons of coral.

Chapter 9
Signs of "Sweet Sixteen"

23 ton "Moon Fountain" with two 18 ton chairs

When you first visit the Coral Castle, you're overwhelmed by the vast amount of objects that you see. You are also aware of a sense of peace that pervades the complex. You feel at home and comfortable, despite the muggy conditions that can sometimes be there.

If you did not know the history of how the Coral Castle eventually arrived at its current Homestead site, you would probably not believe that it was the sole achievement of one 100 pound 5 foot tall Latvian immigrant that spent 20 years or so of his life creating this magnificent structure because of the loss of his "Sweet Sixteen."

This isn't such an unlikely tale. Great achievements have been created based upon the love for a woman. Notably, the Taj Mahal was created after Emperor Shah Jahan, emperor during the Mughal dynasty, was grief stricken when his second wife, Mumtaz Mahal, died during childbirth. This inspired the Emperor to create a monument of his love for his departed wife.

The difference with the story of Emperor Shah Jahan and the story of Ed Leedskalnin is that Emperor Shah Jahan actually was married to his second wife when she died and she had provided 14 children for him.

Ed, on the other hand, theoretically created the Coral Castle for a woman that did not love him, that did not marry him, that did not give him any children, and did not even come to see him after he had created this coral marvel.

Basically, the motivation for Ed creating the Coral Castle, at either the Florida City site or the Homestead site, never made a lot of sense to me.

You might even venture to think that Ed may have been a bit crazy, or even worse, that he had imagined Agnes Scuffs for who in their right mind would believe that a woman would live in a home completely made of stone or lay a baby in a cradle made of solid coral?

This made me think that perhaps Agnes Scuffs was not the entire meaning behind Ed's mysterious "Sweet Sixteen." I began looking for other places at the Coral Castle where the number 16 came up.

I have already stated that the Moon Fountain, with the 6 pointed star in its center, has 16 bevels on the inner lip of the fountain. This shows the relationship between the number 16 and water, the moon, and the 6 pointed star.

I found two other places (and possibly one other), that also have the number 16 associated with them:

1 - There are <u>16 steps</u> leading up to Ed's living quarters

2 - On the <u>metal door</u> at the entrance of the Coral Castle there is a depiction of the Sun and the orbit of the Earth. The sun has 16 rays.

3 - Possibly <u>Ed's well</u> (you cannot count them all, as they disappear beneath the surface of the water.

With these additional reference points, we can come to the following conclusions:

The number 16 could simply represent Ed's "Sweet Sixteen" Agnes, and these are just representative artifacts of his love for her.

Or

The number 16 could represent the secret to his ability to move the enormous stones, which relates to the sun, the moon, the phases of the moon, water, and the 6 pointed star, with the 16 steps to the top of the tower representing levitation itself or energy at a different level.

One other interesting thing to note: the etching on the metal door labels the "Earth" with the <u>number 21</u>. This is very important as it adds to the answer of "Sweet Sixteen" as I will show you later.

Contemplating how all of this was connected, I was drawn for an unknown reason to a strange sculpture that Ed had created near his 243 ton "Tower." Little did I know that this strange little sculpture would become an oracle of many answers, an oracle that I call "The Monkey in the Shells."

Chapter 10
The Monkey in the Shells

Ed's sculpture that I call "The Monkey in the Shells"

For some reason, months later, after having been at the Coral Castle, I began to research geometric figures. Just figures in general, nothing specific. I was inspired after looking at a picture that I had taken of a sculpture that Ed had made near the "Tower" where he lived.

This sculpture is made of cement. In the cement are seashells. Near the middle of this almost trapezoidal sculpture is what appears to be a bright eyed monkey.

I wondered what the significance of "the monkey in the shells" was. I was also wondering at the same time about the significance of the number 16.

So I went to Google and I typed in "seashells" and "16" and hit "enter". This search led me to a website called Patterns in Nature. This website was hosted on Compuserve is now gone, but the following website is similar, discussing the Fibonacci sequence in

Nature or what is commonly called Phi.

The Fibonacci sequence is named after Leonardo of Pisa. It can also be referred to as the Golden Ratio or Phi.

Phi represents the constant number or frequency that all living things operate by. It represents harmony, balance, and growth in a natural healthy environment. You can actually see this demonstrated in these videos: Video 1 (awesome doodling video!) and Video 2.

This website made me think back to what Orval Irwin had said about Ed's response when asked about the 6 pointed star above his bathtub. Ed had responded that he was not Jewish. He said that much of nature is related to the 6 pointed star, such as six pointed snowflakes and perhaps even color blends.

I then wondered if there was a connection?

Did the 6 pointed star and this concept called Phi somehow relate together? Both were directly related to nature. Both were found at the Coral Castle.

I also discovered that Phi had a numeric representation, a numeric constant that pervades not only nature, but mathematics, geometry, and science.

This number is 1.618. Using basic mathematical rules, if you round the "8" up and the "2" down, and ignore the decimal point, you get the number 16.

Could Ed's "Sweet Sixteen" represent a rounded form of the numeric expression of Phi?

This was plausible, but I needed more proof than a simple rounding of numbers. I decided to summarize everything that I had learned so far to see if there was a connection between Phi and Ed's "Sweet Sixteen."

First of all, Ed said that the 6 pointed star was not representative of the Jewish star, but a geometric form found in nature.

At the Florida City site (the original location of the Coral Castle), Ed incorporated the 6 pointed star in various coral pieces, associating it with the moon, the phases of the moon, water, and, of course, coral. <u>All of these things are found in nature</u>.

One coral piece in particular, the 23 ton fountain, with its surrounding crescent moon chairs, has the 6 pointed star in its center, associating the moon, the phases of the moon, water and coral together at the same place. Lining the interior lip of the 23 ton fountain are 16 perfectly formed bevels.

Thus, the number 16 was now related to the 6 pointed star, the moon, the phases of the moon, water, and coral, all things found in nature.

At the Homestead site (the current location of the Coral Castle), Ed again incorporated the number 16 into the steps on his Tower, the rays of the sun on his metal door and possibly his well in the courtyard.

Based upon these re-occurrences of the number 16, and its relationship to the 6 pointed star, I was sure that Phi had something to do with how Ed was able to create the Coral Castle.

Following the lead given to me by the monkey, I decided to see if Ed's "Sweet Sixteen" truly was the mysterious concept of Phi.

Coral Castle Explained   2006-2013 © All Rights Reserved

Chapter 11
Phi in the Stones

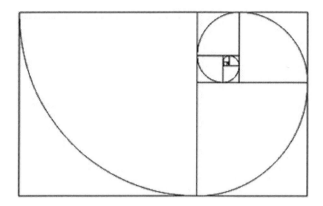

Following my previous researching "skills", I went back to Google and typed "Phi" on my keyboard. There were 3 definitions for Phi. One website defined Phi as the 21st letter of the Greek alphabet. (Remember this number for later!)

Another defined Phi as the Golden Mean, a definition of balance and aesthetic beauty. The other website discussed Phi in mathematical terms, calling it the Golden Ratio. Phi seemed to be incorporated into many aspects of life, but why? And what did this have to do with the Coral Castle?

Remembering that Ed had been quoted as saying that he knew the secrets of the pyramid builders, I wondered if the ancient Egyptians had incorporated Phi into their pyramidal designs.

I found many websites that alluded to how Phi was related to the Great Pyramid of Giza. Moreover, one website showed the relationship of Phi to the royal cubit, the King's chamber and the general dimensions of the Great Pyramid. The more research I did, the more Phi seemed to be connected with almost every aspect of life, specifically aspects that focused on balance, beauty, growth and harmony.

As good as this information was, it still did not answer my questions:

• How was Phi related to the Coral Castle?

• Was Ed's "Sweet Sixteen" a code for the numeric representation of Phi?

• Were the numerous occurrences of 6 pointed star and Phi somehow related?

I decided that the best way to answer all of these questions was through mathematics.
If "Sweet Sixteen" was truly a numeric code, perhaps I could answer all of these questions mathematically.

I decided to follow Ed's lead now, instead of the monkey's, and began to research Phi more deeply.

The first website I found showed how Phi is numerically calculated. The next website showed me that not only was Phi mathematically calculable, but it could be represented geometrically in both spiral and corresponding rectangular grid patterns.

By taking these spiraling and corresponding rectangular grid patterns, and superimposing them over the current outlay of the Coral Castle as depicted on the Coral Castle brochures, I thought that I finally understood the significance of Ed Leedskalnin's "Sweet Sixteen"

Here is the image of the Coral Castle as represented on the brochure from the Coral Castle giftshop:

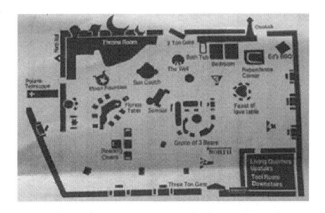

Here is the image of Phi represented as a grid:

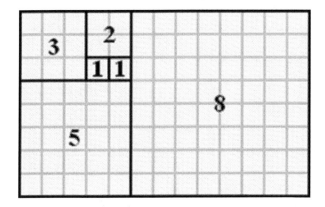

For the sake of this example, I have reversed this image:

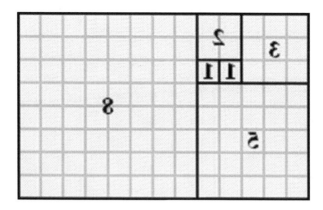

Now, here is the image of Phi represented as a spiral within the grid:

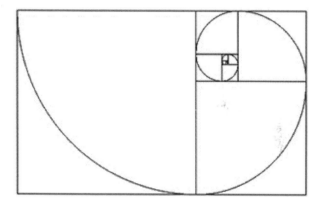

To complete the process, first I will put the Phi grid image superimposed over the image of the Coral Castle from the brochure. Notice how various structures in the Coral Castle seem to line up in the grid representation of Phi:

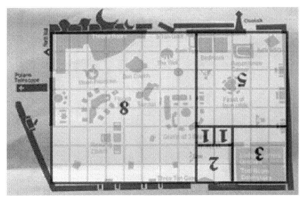

In these images, I have superimposed the spiral representation of Phi over the Coral Castle brochure. Notice how various structures in the Coral Castle seem to follow the spiral representation of Phi.

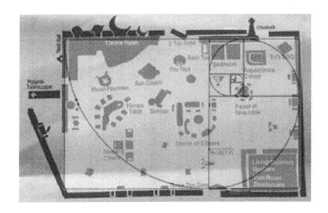

And again inverted...

Coral Castle Explained   2006-2013 © All Rights Reserved

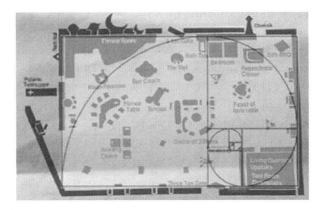

The next image shows how the flow of Phi energy may enter into the Coral Castle, crossing over specific pieces of coral, or the energy may also be generated inside and flow out smoothly due to its Phi based configuration:

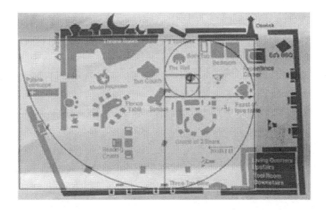

Looking at these simple overlays, it is easy to see that the geometric proportions of the Coral Castle match up with the spiral and grid geometric representations of Phi.

I realized at this point that I was onto something. Phi had to have something to do with how Ed manipulated the coral, and why he configured the Coral Castle to conform with Phi.

I decided to make a summary of what I had discovered so far, and see if I could find any clues toward discovering how Ed utilized Phi and coral together to do the impossible:

Based upon this information, I was able to summarize these 6 key points:

1. Ed related the 6 pointed star to forms found in nature.

2. Phi is a constant found in nature that represents harmony, balance and growth.

3. Phi can be represented numerically as the number 1.618

4. Phi can be represented geometrically in grid and spiral format.

5. <u>Phi is found in ancient architecture</u>, most notably in the construction of the Great Pyramid.

6. Phi can be seen in the rectangular structure of the Coral Castle when the geometric and spiral representations of Phi are overlaid on top of the image of the Coral Castle itself.

After looking at these 6 key points, I came to the following conclusions:

Ed used Phi as the ancient Egyptians did when they built their pyramids. This was the secret of the Egyptians that Ed had rediscovered.

Ed represented Phi at the Florida City site using the 6 pointed star, a pattern found in nature, and at the Homestead site via its rectangular construction and the placement of coral objects within the site itself.

Finally, Ed linked both sites together using the number 16, symbolically at the Florida City site using the 6 pointed star, and mathematically at the Homestead site through its rectangular geometric form.

After linking all of this information together, I was convinced that I had discovered the secret to Ed's "Sweet Sixteen" and the secret that the Egyptian pyramid builders knew thousands of years ago via the concept of Phi.

I say that I "was" convinced because my theory came to an abrupt halt. In fact, I thought I was on the wrong track altogether. Looking at an actual overhead view of the Coral Castle, I realized a great flaw in my theory:

The Coral Castle was not shaped like a rectangle as it was depicted on the brochures. <u>The Coral Castle was square.</u>

Chapter 12
Glitch in the Theory?

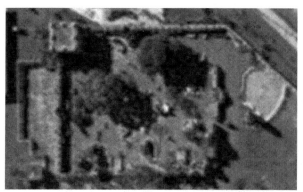

Overhead view of the Coral Castle

I was sure that Ed had created the Coral Castle to represent Phi in a rectangular format. Unfortunately for that, I needed a rectangular form. I remember thinking to myself "I can't be wrong." The patterns are there. The math is there. The repetition of his "Sweet Sixteen" is there. This must be right, but there was something missing.

Following the lead of Pythagoras, who believed that everything was related to mathematics and that numbers were the "ultimate reality," I began to study an overhead image of the Coral Castle. There had to be something that I had missed. While staring at the overhead image of the Coral Castle, I remembered a curious six pointed star chair that was placed near the end of the north wall.

I remembered asking the guides at the Coral Castle why it was there. No one seemed to know. Returning my thinking to the "Monkey in The Shells", I remembered that it was positioned on the south wall near the "Tower" with the embedded monkey staring straight at the end of the north wall.

It was then that I knew that my theory was correct. The "Monkey in The Shells" and this curious 6 pointed star chair made the rectangular connection that I was looking for.

Coral Castle Explained   2006-2013 © All Rights Reserved

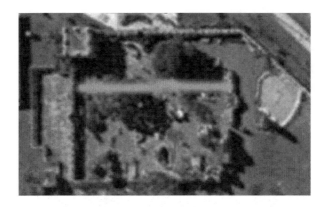

Placing the rectangular representation of Phi into the rectangular area subdivided by the monkey sculpture and the 6 pointed star chair, I finally had found my proof.

This also works proportionately with the Phi spiral, showing once again that the Coral Castle seems to be designed to capture or broadcast Phi based energy.

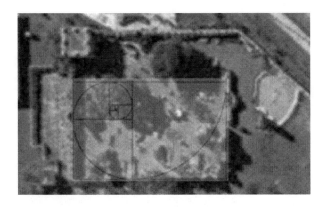

Summarizing what I had just discovered, I doubted very much that all of this could be mere coincidence:

1. The sculpture represented Phi with its many sea shells.

2. The six pointed star represented Phi or "patterns found in nature".

3. And the rectangle created by the two represented the mathematical and geometric representation of Phi.

Even more amazing, Ed had incorporated the squares of the geometric representation of Phi into the Coral Castle as well. Remembering from Chapter 11, the rectangular representation of Phi is based upon the Fibonacci sequence.

The Fibonacci sequence is represented mathematically by the sequence 0,1,1,2,3,5,8,13, etc.

This sequence is represented graphically and geometrically using squares that become the rectangular form of Phi.

While looking at the overhead of the Coral Castle, I noticed that the proportion of the "Tower" and the "Courtyard" seemed to be identical to the proportion of certain squares in the geometric representation of Phi.

Coral Castle Explained   2006-2013 © All Rights Reserved

Using the square representing the number 3, I placed it over the "Tower"

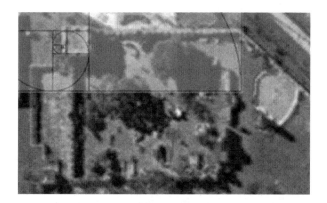

Then I moved the square representing the number 13 over the "Courtyard" area.

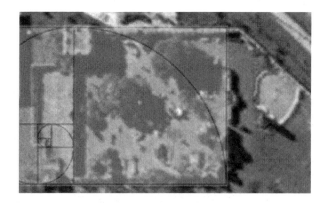

It is seemingly a perfect proportional match. And to add more to this amazing puzzle, when you add the numbers of the two squares that I just used (3 and 13), you get the number 16.

Moreover, the Phi grid and spiral placed over the overhead image of the Coral Castle shows how the Phi spiral flows smoothly in and out over the large pond to the right, and Ed's well.

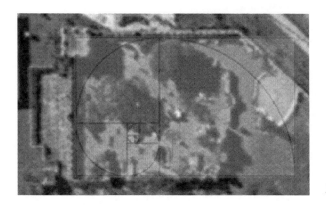

This is very important, as water plays a major role in how Ed was able to create the Coral Castle.

Without a better overhead view, I cannot include decent imagery to show how the Phi spiral connects to many of the other coral pieces in the Coral Castle. It was as if Ed was placing each piece of coral upon the Phi spirals that ran throughout the Coral Castle.

But how could he have known where to place them? What purpose would it serve to do this? I was now more convinced than ever that Ed had intentionally incorporated Phi into the structure of the Coral Castle to lead us closer to the secret of the pyramids that he had deciphered.

What was this secret? Did Phi have some other property other than balance and harmony? Perhaps it enabled Ed to cut, move, and position coral in some way, tapping into some forgotten energy that the ancient stone builders knew about, and that Ed had rediscovered.

Following the trail that seemed to lead toward mathematics, I followed these bread crumbs to a little known form of quantum physics called <u>hyperdimensional physics</u>, a trail that ended with the answer I was looking for.

Chapter 13
Hyperdimensional Physics and Phi

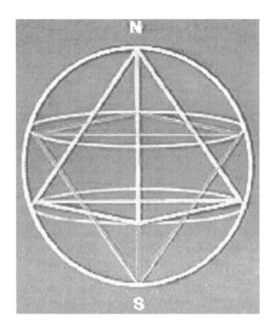

Hyperdimensional physics is a type of physics that was created by Richard C. Hoagland of the Enterprise Mission. Hoagland, a previous science consultant to NASA and Walter Cronkite, is a regular guest on Coast To Coast AM, the largest late-night radio talk show in the world.

Richard Hoagland's hyperdimensional physics theory states that if you take a sphere and place two inverted tetrahedrons inside of it, the apex or peak points of each tetrahedron will touch the sphere at the north and south poles, and the remaining 3 points of each tetrahedron will touch at latitude of 19.5° north and south of the equator.

I wanted to determine if there was a visual correlation proportionate to the latitude of hyperdimensional physics on a sphere and the geometric proof of Phi using the same sphere and hexagonal points.

As I was looking at the many different websites that discussed Phi, I came across one that showed a geometric proof of Phi that involved a circle and a hexagon.

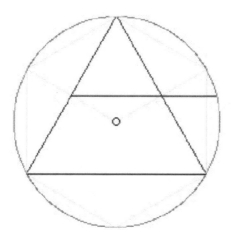

What caught my attention was that by eyeballing the horizontal red line that was used to prove Phi, it seemed to match the same latitude as shown in the images representing hyperdimensional physics.

So I took an image of a sphere with latitudinal lines and superimposed it over the proof of Phi. Then I took Hoagland's hyperdimensional image, and superimposed it over the previous image, and here is what I got:

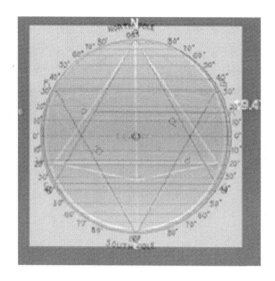

It is almost, using these primitive overlays, a perfect match.

So what does this mean? In my opinion, Phi, the underlying mathematical number that is the basis of harmony, growth and life seems to be directly related to hyperdimensional energy (which is the same as <u>free energy</u>, <u>zero point energy</u>, <u>Chi</u>, etc) which is most notably accessible, on a planetary scale, at the latitude of 19.5°.

Going back to Ed's repetitious use of the 6 pointed star at the Coral Castle, and his statement that it represented structures in nature, his use of this symbol finally made sense to me.

The 6 pointed star not only represented nature, but was also a symbol that represented a mathematical and geometric representation for <u>accessing</u> hyperdimensional or what some call natural earth energy.

As if to confirm this, Ed also associated the Earth itself with Phi. Remember that I mentioned that Ed had labeled the Earth with the number 21 on the metal door?

The 21st letter of the Greek alphabet is Phi, further showing that the Earth, its orbit around the sun, and the natural energy that it generates because of its rotation and orbit, are directly related to the concept of Phi and accessing hyperdimensional energy.

Now that I had a mathematical correlation between hyperdimensional energy and Phi, and an 1100 ton hint from Ed, I needed to know why Ed designed the Coral Castle in the Phi format.

Was it simply a piece of the puzzle, or did the structure of the Coral Castle in some way help attract this hyperdimensional energy into our world? If so, how was Ed able to harness and use this energy to manipulate coral?

I found answers to these questions in the science of vibration and frequency.

Chapter 14
It's in the Geometry, Stupid!

6 pointed star above Ed's bathtub

When I was in college, I took a physics class that had a particularly interesting lab that involved a metal plate, sand, and frequencies with equivalent audible tones.

Based on the work of various scientists including Hans Jenny and Ernst Chladni, in a science that Jenny coined Cymatics, you can see how sound can affect physical matter in a geometric way.

You can click here to see a video of how sound affects matter in geometric patterns.

In the experiment, the metal plate was hooked up to a device that made the vibrations and the vibrations were made audible so that you could hear and see as the sound changed octaves and different geometric patterns formed in the sand.

Each time that the sound levels went up to the next octave, an almost instantaneous change occurred in the sand on the plate. The geometric pattern became more complex as the sound increased in frequency.

This experiment showed me that sound, vibration, frequency, and geometry were all directly related. It also showed me that vibration or frequency could affect physical matter in a geometric way.

Referring back to the geometric proof of Phi and its relationship to hyperdimensional physics, if vibrational frequencies induced a geometric change in physical matter, then you must ask the opposing question:

Do geometric patterns, replicated in physical matter, induce certain frequencies?

As I stated in chapter 11, ancient cultures created structures using Phi. Using these balanced proportions, they created an aesthetic calming effect that was not only visible, but felt in the body.

Likewise, the use of mandalas and labyrinths at many hospitals for the purpose of helping patients heal is becoming a widespread phenomenon.

Feng Shui, an ancient Chinese practice of placement and arrangement of space to achieve harmony with the environment, is also similar to these fields of interest.

It seems that by creating a structure that is based upon the geometry of Phi, the Coral Castle became a place that perpetually resonates with the "feeling" or the frequency of Phi.

Despite the fact that all of this research clearly showed me that physical objects, in the correct geometric configurations, could create a certain "feeling" or field of energy, I still did not know how Ed was able to utilize this energy to manipulate coral as he did.

In essence, the frequency of Phi seemed to open up a gateway to this hyperdimensional energy that Ed was using. However, I did not know where this energy was coming from, or exactly how Ed was accessing it.

My research then led me to another Coral Castle researcher by the name of Ray M. Stoner that looked not only at the positioning of the Coral Castle, but at the source from which Ed drew the energy that he used to create his coral masterpiece.

According to Ray N. Stoner, author of The Enigma of the Coral Castle, Ed was accessing the power of earth energy, or what he calls "etheric energy", from water beneath the ground.

Could this "earth energy" be the same energy that is accessed through hyperdimensional physics? And if so, how could Ed have tapped into it?

In the next chapter, I will discuss how earth energy may be accessed not only through the geometry of the Coral Castle, but actually through the coral itself.

Chapter 15
Water and Earth Energy

Entrance to Ed's well

According to Ray M. Stoner, author of "The Enigma of the Coral Castle", ancient sites around the world that used megalithic stones were often built above flowing channels of water or springs. Famous structures such as Stonehenge in England are known to have many underground water sources, as well as evidence of water at other sites such as the Great Pyramid at Giza and Teotihuacan in Mexico.

According to Stoner's book, water is apparently not only a conduit, but also a storage device for this earth energy.

Before going on, I need to make a distinction at this point:

All of the names that I have used to describe this "unknown" energy source which Ed tapped into using the frequency of Phi go by many names.

Whether you call it hyperdimensional energy, etheric energy, free energy, zero point energy, or chi, this energy is accessible at any time or place, but is most concentrated in areas where the Earth's energy grid, or ley lines are, which carry the highest concentration of this natural Earth energy.

These natural grids can be connecting points between megalithic stones or megalithic structures, but this earth energy is most notably found in underground streams and other sources of underground water.

Therefore, water is a source for high concentrations of this energy, an energy that I will now only refer to as "earth energy", the energy the Ed utilized at the Coral Castle.
Getting back to the main topic, during specific times of the month related to lunar cycles, ancient people were able to harness earth energy that was released during certain lunar phases. This seems to relate directly to the theory of ley lines.

In fact, Stoner mentions that this energy is most accessible at specific times as well, mentioning that it was strongest at the moment that the Sun rose at daybreak.

By first harnessing earth energy, the ancient megalithic builders were able to use this energy to maneuver large blocks of stone over these areas of water to build these ancient sites.

Additionally, by inserting a larger stone into the ground that formed a direct connection with the water below (like Ed's "Obelisk"), the earth energy could be more easily accessed, and even amplified.

The stones would then act not only as tools to help access and amplify the earth energy, but could also be used to add more earth energy to the water below.

Therefore, in ancient times, water, the phases of the moon, and the stone blocks were all interconnected in the gathering, use, and storage of this energy.

So what does this have to do with Ed and his Coral Castle?

Everything.

Looking at the symbology of the coral found at "Ed's Place" and its focus upon nature (the moon, the phases of the moon, water, and the 6 pointed star), it is obvious that he was replicating this same energy system.

- **The 6 pointed star represented Phi and the gateway to the earth energy.**

- **The water represented the source for the earth energy.**

- **The cycles of the moon represented the times when earth energy is most readily available.**

Think about this: before a single piece of coral was put into position, Ed had to have known how to access this earth energy.

Ed incorporated Phi into both the Florida City site and the Homestead site because Phi was the gateway to the earth energy stored in the water.

Building these structures allowed Ed to access, and amplify, the earth energy directly from the water, which in turn allowed him to build larger coral structures and move larger pieces.

We can also assume that, before Ed set up a single block of coral that he was able to access this earth energy at specific times of the month and year, based upon lunar cycles.

And we know exactly when this was because of two of Ed's

largest coral creations:

The Moon Fountain
The Crescent of the East

The Moon Fountain is thought to be a representation of the full moon, and the chairs are representations of 1st quarter moons.

However, the Moon Fountain is actually a representation of the New Moon, and the chairs representative of waning and waxing crescent moons.

The crescent appearance of the moon, and the New Moon, has to do with the absence of direct light on the moon from our perspective.

Essentially, the Sun is behind the moon, and the minimal amount of light that can be seen from our perspective on the Earth gives the moon this appearance.

The Crescent of the East is a representation of the beginning of this 7 day cycle.

Therefore, in my opinion, it is during this time of the month when the Sun and Moon are aligned on the same side of the Earth, giving the Earth a double pull of gravity if you will, that Ed was able to do his work.

So, in summary, we know:

1. **The 6 pointed star represented Phi and the gateway to the earth energy.**
2. **The water represented the source for the earth energy.**
3. **The cycles of the moon represented the times when earth energy is most readily available.**
4. **The 7 days Ed worked represented by the Moon Fountain and the Crescent of the East when this earth energy was**

most readily available.

Yet despite knowing all of this, one question remains:

How was Ed able to access the earth energy from the water to carve and move the blocks of coral to build the Coral Castle?

The answer to this question is found in the study of vibrational resonance.

Chapter 16
Frequencies and Water

Ed's pond

If you have ever played musical instruments, or have taken a basic physics course, you may be familiar with the concept of vibrational resonance. An example of this would be sounding a note on one musical instrument, and then another musical instrument, in the same vicinity, will resonate with that note at the same octave.

So, just as plucking a string on a cello will cause the sounding of a piano chord in the same octave 50 feet away, there had to be a way for Ed to resonate with the earth energy in the water, which would allow him to somehow utilize it to work his megalithic magic.

Then I had a thought ("I'm having a thought, Barbosa", Captain Jack says) Water is about 60% of our body mass. Would it be possible for the water in our bodies to resonate with the water underground? If we could do this, we could tap directly into the earth energy of the water.

What I needed was some supporting evidence that our thoughts and/or our emotions could affect a change in water at a distance. If this were possible, then my example of the cello and piano could be applied from a person to the earth energy in the underground water. My research led me to Dr. Masaru Emoto.

Dr. Masaru Emoto's research has shown that our thoughts and emotions can have an effect on water at a distance, evidenced by the hexagonal (6 pointed) crystalline structure of the ice crystals that are found in the water after freezing.

Dr. Emoto's studies have shown that positive thoughts and emotions sent from a distance can create very symmetrical and beautiful 6 pointed snowflake patterns in the ice.

In fact, the more positive the thoughts and emotions, the more beautiful and complex the 6 pointed snowflake pattern would become.

Alternately, negative thoughts and emotions sent from a distance would distort the 6 pointed crystalline structure of the ice so much that the ice crystals no longer remotely resembled a snowflake pattern.

These studies show us that our thoughts and emotions can have a direct effect on water at a distance. Therefore, based upon Dr. Emoto's research and findings, we can make the following conclusions:

1 - If Phi represents the underlying frequency of life, balance, and beauty in nature, and the 6 pointed star represents a symbolic and mathematic representation of the gateway to earth energy (hyperdimensional energy, chi, zero point, etc), then by maintaining a mindset and emotional state that is positive and balanced, we should be able resonate with the earth energy in the water.

2 – The reason that Ed used the symbol of the 6 pointed star so many times at the Coral Castle, many times in connection with coral objects adjacent to water (Ed's bathtub, the Obelisk embedded 6 feet into the ground, etc) was because it is a symbolic representation of the frequency or state of someone in a perfectly balanced or Phi state of mind.

Therefore, by being in a Phi state of mind, or being in the midst of a structure that resonates at the Phi frequency, we can automatically and easily tap into this natural earth energy in the water because the water in our bodies will resonate with the earth energy in the water underground.

Now that I knew that being in a balanced or Phi state of mind is the key to tapping into natural earth energy, I needed to answer two more questions:

1 – We knew how to connect to the Earth energy in the water, but what about connecting to the coral itself?

2 - How did Ed use this energy to manipulate the massive pieces of coral?

To discover how Ed could connect with the coral, I had to understand a little more about what coral actually was. And in doing so, I was able to finally understand the connection between Giza and the Coral Castle, the reason why Ed said he knew the secrets of the pyramid builders.

Chapter 17
The Giza Coral Castle Connection

The Great Pyramid of Giza and Ed's Tower

Now that I had confirmed, through the research of Dr. Masuro Emoto, that we could connect with the natural Earth energy in the water, I needed to know how Ed was able to affect a physical change on the coral.

My reasoning was that if our ability to connect with the water was based upon the water content in our own bodies, we could only connect with the coral if we had coral within us.

Although this seemed ridiculous, I needed to find a catalyst, a connection between ourselves and the coral if my theory was to make sense. I decided to find out exactly what coral was made of.

First, I started to learn about the nature of coral and how it was actually formed.

Coral is made from a substance called oolite. Oolite is a sedimentary rock formed from what are called Ooids. Ooids are small spheres that are mostly composed of **calcium carbonate**.

Calcium carbonate is a substance that is secreted by the corals or polyps which are the little animals that actually live in the coral reefs. The coral reefs grow as the polyps and other organisms deposit calcium carbonate which creates the coral reefs themselves.

So to summarize: a coral reef is the result of small creatures called corals or polyps that secrete calcium carbonate which creates the coral reefs. This later becomes oolitic limestone which is what most of southern Florida is actually made of.

Now let me give you one more definition which will help you tie all of this in...
Another definition for coral is this: **a coral reef or limestone structure that was produced by living organisms.** Limestone is a type of rock composed primarily of the mineral calcite (another important word to remember) which is the crystalline form of calcium carbonate.

So what does this have to do with the Great Pyramids of Giza?

The Great Pyramid of Giza was built with an estimated 2.3 million limestone blocks composed primarily of the mineral calcite, the crystalline form of calcium carbonate which is the same material that makes a coral.

Here is a quick summary:

- **Polyps secrete calcium carbonate**
- **Calcium carbonate creates the coral**
- **The crystalline form of calcium carbonate is calcite**
- **Limestone is made of calcite**
- **Limestone = coral**

So there is our connection. The oolitic limestone, the coral that Ed

Leedskalnin used to build his Coral Castle is made up of the same skeletal coral structures that the limestone at the Great Pyramid of Giza was made from. **The stones, though given different names, are in composition absolutely identical.**

So then you may ask what does this have to do with the secrets of the pyramids builders? What can the similarities between the constitutions of both coral and limestone have to do with Ed's ability to move 1100 tons of coral without the aid of modern machinery?

Earlier I had mentioned that both coral and limestone share a common mineral. It is called calcite. Calcite, the crystalline form of calcium carbonate, is the primary component of both coral and limestone. http://en.wikipedia.org/wiki/Quartz

Calcite is part of what is called the Trigonal Crystal system. And within the system is what is called a hexagonal lattice system. Quartz also is part of this same trigonal crystal system, and as we all know, quartz is use for many purposes, including the transmission of radio signals and the processing of information in computers.

I wondered if the human body naturally produced calcite, and if it did, if it could be used in some way by the human brain, acting as a transmitter of our intentions, and the earth energy, to affect a change in the coral?

My research led me to something I did not expect. It led me to a little known organ in the human brain called the Pineal gland.

Chapter 18
Calcite and the Pineal Gland

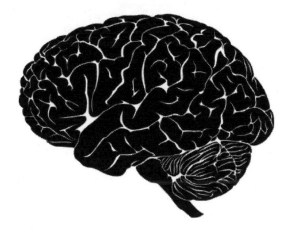

The Human Brain

Now that I knew quartz and calcite shared a similar crystalline configuration and that if quartz is able to act as a catalyst for conveying information, much like a silicon computer chip that we use today in our computers, why couldn't calcite act in a similar manner?

My research led me to looking at the pineal gland, and as you will see at the end of this chapter, it is the perfect catalyst for connecting with the calcite in the coral.

The pineal gland is a small organ situated at the exact center of the brain between the left and right hemispheres. It has been thought by scientists to be an evolutionary leftover, however many others believe it to be much more than that.

Going back as far as the ancient Greeks, all the way up to modern definitions, the pineal gland has been associated in shape to the pinecone, hence the reason for its name.

In fact, the pinecone has been used symbolically in history throughout many different cultures. It is seen in the staff of Osiris from the Egyptian culture. In the Sumerian culture, by Babylon God Tamus holding a pinecone for some type of ritual.

There is even a large pinecone at the Vatican and on a rod that the Pope holds. Even the great philosopher Descartes wrote about it calling it the seat of the soul, the connection between God and man.

But even more interestingly, especially to me, the pinecone has mathematical implications with its relationship to the Fibonacci sequence and Phi.

So how would the Pineal gland help us connect with the coral stones?

In science, the pineal gland does not simply reside at the base of the two hemispheres of the brain, but also resides at the base of the thalamus, the organ whose functions include relaying sensation, spatial sense, and motor signals to the cerebral cortex.

The thalamus also regulates consciousness, sleep, and alertness. Combined with the fact that it is directly tapped into our nervous system, and is in charge of the regulation of our circadian rhythm, it is the perfect biological time piece, our very own quartz crystal that resides within our brain.

Going back to the correlation between calcite and quartz, I realized that if the pineal gland truly was some kind of transmitter for our intentions, and if it could harness the energy of the earth to help Ed move the coral blocks, connecting with the calcite in the coral, there had to be some research that related to my theory.

In a recent study, it has been shown that the pineal gland contains a new form of biomineralization similar to the production of the biologically created magnetite crystals within our human brain.

What has been found in the pineal gland is calcite.

Based on the fact that pineal gland contains calcite, and due to its location in the brain, it is my belief that Edward Leedskalnin was able to carve, mold and levitate the coral by connecting directly with the calcite in the coral using the earth energy in the water while in a Phi state of mind.

Now that I had a connection between a human being and the coral blocks, I only had one more question: how was he able to manipulate the coral once the connection was made?

The answer to this lies in the science of morphogenetic fields and the concept of intention.

Chapter 19
Morphogenetic Fields and Intent

The 30+ ton "Crown", North Wall of the Coral Castle

The work of Rupert Sheldrake regarding morphogenetic or "morphic fields", presents the hypothesis that the universe has a basic set of archetypes, similar to those postulated by Carl Jung and also similar to Plato's theory of forms.

According to Sheldrake, by doing certain actions, with certain feelings and intentions in a repetitious matter, morphic fields can be created.

Moreover, these morphic fields can be accessed by all others, giving them access to the thoughts, actions, and energy of all those that have ever accessed these fields before.

In order to access a morphic field that has been created, all one has to do is feel the frequency or "feeling" of these morphic fields and this allows you to access any morphic field that you desire.

This is similar to the research of Gregg Braden and his concept of "feeling" with intention, that is discussed in the book <u>The Divine Matrix</u>, in order to manifest a change in physical reality.

Braden gives an example of how some Native American cultures will do a rain dance. In order to manifest a rain storm, the people will intend a rainstorm to occur by "feeling" as if the rainstorm was already there. They will imagine in their minds and feel with their bodies that "feeling" of rain falling upon them, their feet already in puddles of water.

By creating this "feeling" of a rainstorm, they are actually accessing the morphic field of manifesting rainstorms, and the earth energy now has a mechanism by which to manifest their intent for rain.

Also related to this would be accessing the morphic fields of healing that <u>Dr. Eric Pearl</u>, or <u>Dr. Richard Bartlett</u> have access to. They are able to feel a certain feeling, a certain frequency, and by doing so they are able to access a morphic field that can heal people.

In relation to Ed, I believe that he was able to go into the Phi state of mind and access or remember the "feeling" associated with the morphic fields used by the ancient megalithic stone builders.

Doing this gave him the ability to access and utilize the natural earth energy in the water which allowed him to cut, move and position these enormous blocks of coral and create the Coral Castle by connecting to the calcite in the coral via the pineal gland.

The problem with this theory is that Ed would have had to have known the frequency or "feeling" of this morphic field in order to access it. The question is how did he discover the frequency of this morphic field?

I believe that Ed discovered this feeling for the morphic field of the ancient stone builders purely by accident. I believe that Ed acquired this "feeling" through a near death experience.

Chapter 20
How Ed Got "The Power"

Famous "9 Ton Gate" on east wall

Throughout history, there are many examples of people accidentally accessing knowledge of great value that they did not understand, but then found a way to rationalize it and apply it to the "real world".

The physicist Francis Crick, who won the Nobel Peace Prize for his discovery of the double helix structure of DNA, confessed near the time of his death that he had actually discovered the double helix structure while on an LSD trip. Albert Einstein figured out the theory of relativity while imagining riding on a beam of light. He then back engineered his imaginary ride into a mathematical formula, which led inevitably to the theory of relativity.

The structure of the benzene ring was discovered by Friedrich

Kekule while having a dream and saw a vision of serpents that formed into the hexagonal pattern of what we now call the benzene ring. There are many more stories, and one that I heard personally not too long ago...

Dr. Richard Bartlett once shared a story of a student of his that went to Machu Picchu and was able to enter into the morphic field of levitating stones. He was simply wondering how the builders of Machu Picchu originally moved the megalithic stones that were there.

He went into an open access state (a relaxed or Phi state of mind) in order to get a connection or a "feeling" to the stones. After doing this, within moments, he heard a tone in his mind, and the stone that he was focusing upon lifted up 6 inches off the ground. This person, a school teacher, was able to accidentally tap into the morphic field of moving megalithic stones because he had entered into an altered state of consciousness.

In the same way, relating back to the story that Ed was found nearly dead in Florida City by the Moser family, it is my belief is that when Ed nearly died from his tuberculosis that he had a near death experience.

It is my opinion that Ed experienced an altered state of consciousness during a near death experience which tapped him into that morphic field that allows you to magically move and manipulate enormous limestone or coral rocks.

This morphic field could have been created by the indigenous American Indians in the Florida area that were responsible for creating such structures as the Miami Circle that was discovered nearly a decade ago.

This could have been the same morphic field that all ancient megalithic stone builders like the ancient Egyptians and the builders of Stonehenge tapped into thousands of years ago.

Whatever he did, or however he came about this amazing ability, the evidence, pun intended, is "set in stone" AKA the Coral Castle itself.

From this perspective, I began to see why Ed did what he did. I began to see from his eyes.

In the next chapter, I will give you my assessment of Ed Leedskalnin's journey, from obscurity to the miraculous.

Chapter 21
A Journey to Discovery

Nearly 30 ton Polaris Telescope

The following account is my interpretation of what Ed may have done after acquiring his new powers. Although this is complete speculation on my part, I think that it follows a very logical path of discovery.

After recovering from tuberculosis, Ed now had an amazing ability that he did not have before. Like a child with a new toy, Ed began to ask questions. Perhaps his new found powers worked sometimes and not others. He may have realized that he had to be in a calm state to access this energy, and that certain phases of the moon helped and others did not.

Ed may have begun to look for answers at the library. He may have seen symbols during his near death experience, the geometric kind that are often reported during altered states of consciousness. He may have realized that the visions he saw matched symbols and numbers from ancient Egypt.

His ability to move and carve these enormous stones led him to the history of the Egyptians and other ancient megalithic structures, and he realized that they had similar knowledge. At this point, Ed decided to create his own megalithic structure, not only to represent his new powers and amplify his energy, but also for his "Sweet Sixteen", the one that he originally loved.

Over time, after moving from Florida City, he decided to do as the Egyptians did. After realizing his "Sweet Sixteen" from Latvia would never come, he decided to leave a legacy behind, a great puzzle, a map to discover his knowledge. A map of coral, embracing his new "Sweet Sixteen", that would last forever.

I believe that Ed had been planning this move for years. How else could he have coordinated the cutting, moving, and positioning of 1100 tons of coral in less than four years, and 900 tons in less than two years?

Once he was settled at Homestead, he began to make astronomical and electromagnetic discoveries and wrote about the discoveries that he made. Over time he discovered how the Earth rotated using his sundial, represented by the analemma "figure 8" etchings on the sundial itself. Ed also learned that he could access the natural earth energy in an unnatural way.

Understanding that it took human attenuation in a Phi state of mind to access this natural energy located in the water and access the morphic field for manipulating megalithic stones, Ed found a way to access it without needing to enter a Phi state of mind.

Ed created a perpetual motion machine that could access the earth energy without human intention or the human mind. Upon completing his work, he wrote pamphlets, made multiple diagrams and even created a prototype that still sits in his tool room today.

All of Ed's discoveries were initiated by a chance step into the unknown, tapping him into the energetic fields of the indigenous tribes that were perhaps related to the Miami Circle builders, or the megalithic stone builders of the world. Either way, his experience demanded answers, and these answers were written by Ed into the stones at the Coral Castle.

With all of this said, perhaps the most amazing part of Ed's journey of discovery was not made during his life, but after his death. All of Ed's energy, along with his ability to tap into the natural earth energies and morphic fields, seems to have created another morphic field that he had not anticipated.

In the next chapter, I will discuss what I call my "unexpected encounter".

Chapter 22
An Unexpected Encounter

Picture of Ed at the Coral Castle

Although I initially was not going to add this chapter to the book, I felt that it is an important part of why I may have written this book at all. I believe that Ed may have created the ultimate morphic field. I believe that Ed Leedskalnin is still at the Coral Castle.

Ideas of quantum physics, quantum entanglement, and morphic fields have always been an interest of mine, as they give credence to the possibility of unseen energy fields that may possess some level of intent or even consciousness.

On my first day at the Coral Castle, after going through about a 45 minute tour with the tour guide John, I decided to go up into the Tower, which is the 243 ton quarters that Ed built that served as both his tool room and his residency.

Climbing the 16 steps to the top, I crossed the threshold of the doorway and was, for lack of a better or more correct adjective, struck by some wall of energy. It came from the front, enveloped me, and made me drop to my knees and teeter backwards.

I grabbed outward to the side of the doorway for support. I felt myself blacking out. I also remember what I can only describe as a kind of cool heavy electricity going through me. It was like being punched with an enormous electrical boxing glove that also started to squeeze.

Fighting off the blackout I shook my head. Someone helped me to my feet. I maintained my balance holding onto the side of the doorway. When I focused my eyes, the cardboard figure that Leedskalnin, dressed in his finest suit, stared back at me on the other side of the rail that divided the general public from his remaining effects including his chair, bed, and a few other personal items.

After a few minutes, I felt much better. I took some time to look around the little area where Ed lived. A series of pictures were taken (which I will discuss in the next chapter), including a picture of me standing near the cardboard version of Ed.

I did not know what force had hit me. It was similar to feelings I have had going into areas that are purportedly haunted. Whatever this energy was, it was much more powerful than anything I had experienced before.

One possibility is that the energy could have been related to the construction of the Coral Castle itself. Perhaps earth energy naturally builds in the upper area of the Tower which could be why Ed slept upstairs.

Regardless of the infinite possibilities of what the energy could have been, I personally believe that I accidentally ran into the morphic field of Ed himself or, at the very least, the residue of his energetic form. The reason that I am putting this in the book is because up until recently, I had no way of confirming that this energy was real.

I had heard from the guides at the Coral Castle that various people throughout the years had felt some kind of energy in the upper room of the Tower. Then, accidentally, I ran across a website that confirmed my experience using modern technology.

Chapter 23
Measurement of a Ghost

Energy captured in corner of Ed's room

In the last chapter, I had mentioned that a picture had been taken of me next to the cardboard picture of Ed in the upper room of the Tower. What I did not mention was that not all of the pictures that were taken in Ed's room came out normal.

Specifically, five or six pictures that we took in the southeast and southwest corners (those are the corners at the back of Ed's room when you walk in) did not come out at all. (see above image)

Here is an image that came out:

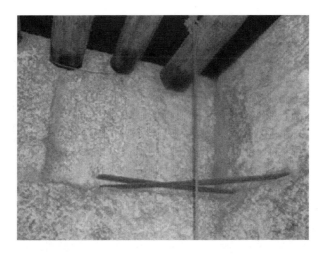

I tried to take images of the corners from various angles, thinking that it was a lighting problem. Almost every image came out distorted. Finally, I went near the corners (you can't actually get to two of the corners. They are blocked off by a rail) and could feel a strange energy, similar to what I felt at the door before, but less intense.

I thought that this energy was concentrated in the upper corners about six or 7 feet up, near strange recesses and bars in the coral blocks, yet I had no way of measuring what I thought to be there. I had no way of testing this hypothesis. It could have just been in my mind as I had no way of empirically measuring what I felt.

Then one day, while looking for a clear image of the 16 steps that lead up to the upper room of the Coral Castle tower, I found the PRISM Paranormal Investigations website.

This group did a paranormal investigation of the upper room of the Tower after hearing from the Coral Castle staff that another paranormal research team had investigated the property in the past and noticed unusually high EMF levels in the living quarters.

Although you can find this website on Google, this page seems to have been moved to another area of their site. The PRISM researchers did their own test and noticed an EMF spike of approximately 1 to 2 mG occurred across the top part of the metal railing around the room, exactly where I had sensed that the energy was the strongest!

Suffice to say, I was very happy. I felt vindicated and not so crazy. Although this may not prove to anyone that Ed or Ed's energy is in that room, it clearly shows that there is an abnormal amount of electromagnetic energy in the southeast and southwest corners, an energy that felt, to me, like a ghost.

In the next chapter, I am going to discuss a mystery that has existed regarding a certain set of numbers that Ed Leedskalnin left behind at the Coral Castle. These numbers are thought to be the "secret to the universe". Fortunately, these numbers can actually be explained.

Chapter 24
Ed's Last Words?

Famed "Secret to the Universe" in Ed's room

Many people that have studied the lore of the Coral Castle may have heard of a series of numbers that Ed Leedskalnin had written that were purportedly the "Secret to the Universe" in mathematical form. This series of numbers was supposedly on a plaque above Ed's bed and was entitled, "The Secret to the Universe is... 7129/6105195."

I had heard of this amazing number for years prior to going to the Coral Castle. I had seen many websites that tried to decipher Ed's numerical secret. To the knowledge of the guides at the Coral Castle, there was never a plaque above Ed's bed that had stated anything about a secret to the universe.

However, the numbers were in Ed's living quarters. This part was true. Scrawled or etched into the coral as you walk out of the doorway of Ed's living quarters are what look like the numbers 7129/6105195.

I initially thought that this set of numbers had some mathematical significance. The work of Jeremy Stride at Code144.com made me believe there is was some significance to the numbers.

However, Jeremy contacted me on the way to the Coral Castle a few years ago, and found out the true meaning of Ed's numbers and shot a video that explains the secret of Ed's numbers in less than 30 seconds.

Sometimes unexplained numbers are simply unexplainable. And sometimes, as in this case, there is a perfectly logical explanation:

Ed's Immigration Papers

On the Internet, there is a video image of Ed's immigration document. On the document, you will see these 2 numbers:

Petition # - 7129
Immigration Certificate # - 6105195

As you can see, there is a logical explanation for the numbers that have been regarded by many as the "secret to the universe". Unfortunately, the rest of the mystery is not as easy to figure out.

One of the most intriguing aspects of Ed Leedskalnin is a device he left behind that sits in the Tool Room. It was once thought to be a perpetual motion machine.

The next chapter discusses what this device might be, and how Ed may have used it to create the Coral Castle. And it may also be what inevitably led to his death...

Chapter 25
Why Ed Died

Remnants of Ed's Perpetual Motion Machine

A guest on Coast to Coast AM by the name of Stewart Swerdlow mentioned the he had been part of something called the Montauk project and the Philadelphia experiment several decades ago. Stewart had mentioned that thousands of people were used as human guinea pigs for government experiments with electromagnetic energy. Sadly, most of the people that were used in these experiments did not survive due to prolonged exposure to electromagnetic fields.

Even today, fears regarding cancer, power lines, and even cell phones are a definite area of concern regarding the ill effects that can occur when a person is exposed to electromagnetic energy for an extended period of time.

I believe that Ed, unaware of the harm that he was doing to his body while experimenting with his electromagnetic free energy device, became an unknowing guinea pig for his own experiments, and died as a result of complications from his prolonged exposure.

The remnants of Ed's antigravity device are in his tool shed, directly below his living quarters.

If this is where he operated this device when it was operational, it would have been in a prime location to assault his body with huge doses of electromagnetic radiation.

Orval Irwin's book "Mr. Can't Is Dead" recounts a time when the local police were called in to investigate why Ed was stringing copper wire from the tips of his tallest coral pieces. Ed reportedly said it was for his radio. I am sure it had to do with something else.

I believe that Ed was trying to create a way to access free energy for everyone, much like [Nikoli Tesla](), regardless if they had the Phi mindset or not. Instead of harnessing free energy naturally through the body, Ed was trying to create a device that could provide access to this energy without the use of the mind.

In Ed's own pamphlets, he discusses what he calls his "Perpetual Motion Holder" which is a device that would run forever and never run out of energy. The remnants of this device, though inoperable today, may have been the reason that Ed Leedskalnin died in 1951.

But if it did work, what is missing from this device now that would make it operable once again?

Many people have thought that Ed was working with counter rotating fields. This is a popular notion due to the work of scientist like [David Sereda]() and John Hutchinson. David Sereda is famous for several accomplishments, one of which being his work with stone technology.

David is able to program stones with what he calls "harmonic codes" which are differentials that he has mathematically determined by measuring each face of the six sided quartz crystal, and dividing by the adjacent side, this result gave him the mathematical frequency for the crystal itself.

John Hutchinson is famous for the Hutchinson Effect in which he uses high-frequency radio waves and a Tesla coil to raise the frequency of the physical object until it begins to float.

However, in the area of counter rotating fields, two rotating discs of different diameters are spun, one clockwise, the other counterclockwise. These electromagnetically charged disks are able to create a measurable reduction in the perceived mass of objects between them, most notably in the experiments done by Eugene Podkletnov.

It is my assumption that the reason Ed's device no longer works is because the other rotating disk is now missing. However, if this was the technology Ed was working with, it begs a simple question:

Regardless of the success of Eugene Podkletnov, if Ed was working toward producing a device that could replicate his abilities, allowing people to instantly enter a Phi state of mind, why would Ed be working with counter rotating fields?

The answer is that the natural energy field of the body is also a counter rotating field.

Chapter 26
Merkabah and Hemispheric Synchronization

The Tetrahedral 3 Ton Gate

Ed's work into counter rotating fields at the end of his life was perplexing to me. I believe that he was trying to create a device that would allow people to enter a Phi state of mind in order to do what he was able to.

But what did counter rotating fields have to do with the human body and energy system? What was I missing? Was there any religious or cultural belief that involved the human energy system, counter rotational fields and any of the symbology that Ed had used at the Coral Castle? My research led me to something called Merkabah mysticism.

Merkabah or Merkavah is a type of Jewish mysticism based upon the Book of Ezekiel. It is the word used in the Hebrew to describe a heavenly vehicle that Ezekiel saw in the sky. Merkabah is also defined as a spirit light body and is depicted as a three dimensional six pointed star (2 tetrahedrons merged together) surrounded by counter rotating fields of energy.

In some teachings, the Merkabah was an interdimensional vehicle, a gateway to God, a description that seems oddly similar to the description of the pineal gland being the "seat of the soul" giving us access to the divine.

The correlation of Ed's frequent use of the six pointed star and Ed's Flywheel that produced counter rotational fields of energy is uncanny.

If the human body truly does have counter rotating fields of energy surround it, then perhaps the key to helping people reach a Phi state of mind is not done by creating a counter rotational field of energy, but perhaps it is as simple as showing them how to balance their own.

If the pineal gland is truly a gateway to the divine, residing at the exact center of the two hemispheres of our brain, just as the Great Pyramid of Giza resides at the exact center of the Earth's land mass, then perhaps the key to accessing the Earth's hyperdimensional energy begins with balancing the hemispheres of our mind.

HemiSync

Hemi-Sync is a technology that utilizes audio sound patterns that work to synchronize both hemispheres of the brain. Robert Monroe of the Monroe Institute developed this technology for his students in an attempt to help them achieve similar results that he had achieved in regard to out of body experiences and lucid dreams.

This technology utilizes what are called binaural beats. Essentially, two different tones are played in each ear, causing the brain to create an auditory processing artifact which sounds like a pulsating tone.

This artifact is a result of the two hemispheres of the brain synchronizing together.

If our body truly does have counter rotating fields of energy, by using this technology, it would be possible to balance this energy, thus creating a Phi state of mind.

In the same way that counter rotating fields of energy are created by two rapidly spinning disks of different sizes spinning in opposite directions, it is possible that the two different tones are actually causing the same type of effect in the human energy system, thus effectively creating a gateway to the hyper dimensional earth energy I have been referencing.

Ed seemed to be trying to create a way for people to do what he did through his experiments in counter rotating fields. Though I believe this form of technology eventually led to his death, it is possible that Hemi Sync technology may hold the key to helping people do what Ed did.

If that sounds ridiculous to you, let me share a personal story that may conclusively show that all of what I have presented, the ability of a human being to manipulate coral with their mind and intentions, may actually be possible.

Chapter 27
How We Can Do What Ed Did

North Wall and the Throne Room

Although I have never levitated a single stone, nor do I personally know the feeling of this morphic field, a personal experience that allowed me to heal a little girl suffering from spinal scoliosis, and the impending surgery that was supposed to fix her, is what I would like to share with you.

Haley is my friend's daughter. She had been walking pigeon toed for a number of months. She was also having back pain. She was taken to a Shriners hospital and was diagnosed with scoliosis.

She was subsequently taken to a specialist who concurred with the diagnosis. A visual examination and two x-rays were done to confirm an 8° bend in her spine.

I have done hands-on healing and distance healing for 20 years. I offered to try to help her not knowing if I could. Her mother and I sat with her and we did a healing on this little girl two days before she was set to go in to determine if she would wear a back brace or go in for surgery.

She was taken in for a third x-ray two days after her healing, and that x-ray revealed that there was no bend in her spine. The scoliosis was gone!

The reason that I am bringing this story to your attention is that what occurred with Haley's spine is no different than what Ed did when moving the blocks.

When I do a healing, I always clear my mind, and enter a Phi state of mind, where I am completely balanced. I then remember the feeling of healing, and think of what I would like to have healed. Once that intention has been thought or stated, I let go, getting out of the way.

Every healer knows that you must, in a sense, move out of the picture. The power that heals is not yours, but is an energy that comes through you, and moves toward the intention that you have in mind.

The reason that this is such a good example is that bone tissue, specifically the hard compact bone that forms the outer portion of the spine is called bone mineral, a form of hydroxyapatite.

Hydroxylapatite or hydroxyapatite is a naturally forming calcium-based mineral which is one of the few minerals produced and used by biological systems like the human body.

When it hardens, it crystallizes in the hexagonal crystal system and is based upon the hexagonal lattice system, the same crystalline system that we discussed in relation to both quartz crystals and calcite.

So in the same way that Ed was able to connect with and

manipulate the coral, I was able to affect a positive change for this little girl by connecting with her spine while accessing the morphic field of healing.

Haley is now 5 inches taller and a happy popular 13 year old that walks normally. She no longer has to wear casts on her legs which she had to for the pigeon toed walking. And the scoliosis is also gone.

Based upon my personal experience with manipulating the calcium based minerals in her spine, I am sure that, if we could ever discover the morphic field of levitating stones, that feeling that Ed felt over 70 years ago, we could also levitate megalithic blocks of stone.

On the Coral Castle website, it says that when people asked Ed how he created the Coral Castle "Ed would only say that he knew the secrets used to build the ancient pyramids and if he could learn them, you could too."

Based upon my research, and based upon my personal experience with healing Haley's spine, I would have to say that Ed was right.

Now let's look at a summary of why the Coral Castle is so important...

Chapter 28
Why the Coral Castle Is Important

Replica of Stonehenge Menhir stone

If you ever visit the Miami area in South Florida, it is guaranteed that you will see in your hotel lobby many pamphlets for the uncountable attractions available to every tourist. There are pamphlets for tours of Miami, the Miami Sea aquarium, and various other attractions, all aimed at having fun in the sun.

And in the midst of these is another attraction: the Coral Castle. Placing a pamphlet for the Coral Castle amidst all of the other attractions is not a bad idea. In fact, it is a great way to get people from all over the world to see this magnificent structure. The problem is that unless you are a visitor, you more than likely will never know what an amazing feat of engineering that Ed created all by himself so many years ago.

The Coral Castle is simply equated with being an attraction and not a megalithic structure of unbelievable proportions because of where it is located. In this chapter, I would like to point out three things that make the Coral Castle one of the most important structures on the face of the planet Earth.

It is important not only as a remarkable achievement, but because of what it represents in regard to the near future of mankind.

First, the Coral Castle was built in contemporary times, less than 100 years ago.

This means that the megalithic achievements that we see all around the world, such as Stonehenge in England and the great Pyramids of Giza, are not merely things of the past, but are replicable structures that can also be made today.

Second, the Coral Castle was created by one man, Edward Leedskalnin.

The fact that Ed created the Coral Castle by himself means that the theories regarding the necessity of thousands of slaves, or the use of primitive tools to build these structures, are no longer valid.

Third, Ed created a structure that has direct access to zero point energy.

Call it whatever you will, zero point energy, chi, or hyperdimensional energy, whatever its name, it is the same energy source from which all things were and are made.

In this world of dwindling resources, the ability to find a new source of energy is very much in demand. The Coral Castle is a testament to Ed's ability harness, amplify and utilize this energy in our world.

This field of energy can be felt just by visiting the Coral Castle. Just by being there, it can help rebalance your energy. It resonates at the frequency of Phi, amplified by the Coral Castle itself.

If all of us could learn to tap into this energy, we would not only have access to unlimited free energy, and have the ability to start shaping our own lives by tapping into the morphic fields of our choice through our personal intent and focus.

Studies by [Dean Radin](#) and [Lynne McTaggart](#) have shown that intent is a very powerful force in the universe and if harnessed, has the ability to change the past, present, and future.

Perhaps, in these end times, this great megalithic structure, the Coral Castle, is a starting point for all of us wanting to tap into natural earth energies and morphic fields to begin to reshape our world for the better.

In the last and final chapter, I leave you with the question you should be asking after reading the last 23 chapters...

Conclusion
So Now What?

Ed's Sundial

Now that you have read about the secrets of the Coral Castle, you might be asking yourself "Now what?" It isn't that I have described how Ed created the Coral Castle, and that is the end of the story. The story is open ended, and you are the next part of the story.

The Coral Castle was created by Ed Leedskalnin as a tool to help anyone visiting, to resonate with the frequency of Phi. Having the ability to tap directly into the Earth's natural energy, someone should be able to find the "feeling" that Ed did and tap into the morphic field of the megalithic stone builders.

But the Coral Castle is about much more than moving large stones.

I believe that all forms of the miraculous are done by going into the Phi state, and tapping into particular morphic fields that allow us to do magical things. Through experimentation at the Coral Castle, or by tapping into the morphic field of the Coral Castle itself, it should help anyone tap into the unknown.

Coral Castle Explained   2006-2013 © All Rights Reserved

Let me conclude this book with one more personal story...

In Dr. Richard Bartlett's book Matrix Energetics, he teaches a technique called a "two point" which allows you to access the morphic field of healing, the same energy I used to heal my own DVT (Deep Vein Thrombosis) and heal Haley from scoliosis.

One day, my little girl, Olivia, and I sat down together to test out Dr. Bartlett's initial exercises. To make a long story short, Olivia learned his "two point" method with me in under 10 minutes.

Using it on my head, she was able to knock out a migraine headache that I had had all day on her first try. All I told her to do was "think a happy thought" and the magic occurred. Why a happy thought? Happy thoughts are usually thought by those who are balanced and that resonate in a Phi state of mind.

Ed created the Coral Castle to make it easier to tap into this Phi state, which is the doorway to the infinite energies and possibilities of the universe. Just being at the Coral Castle gives you a feeling of harmony and peace because the frequency of Phi radiates all around you.

In my opinion, it is our job to use Ed's creation to further our understanding of morphic fields and other realities. He didn't just create the Coral Castle as a sideshow. He created it so we all can begin to tap into the infinite.

In regard to scientific studies, I believe that further studies need to be done at the Coral Castle, regarding the alignment of the complex and getting GPS readings on every stone at the castle.

The Coral Castle is well taken care of, but what needs to be done now is a thorough scientific study, just as scientists have done with other ancient megalithic sites around the world.

At the very least, the Coral Castle should be looked at as a sacred megalithic site. People should go there just to balance their body's energies, and potentially tap into the morphic fields of healing, success, or just happiness.

The Coral Castle is Ed's gift to us. A message in stone, hidden in plain sight, to help all of us begin to change ourselves and our world. It is a gift that all of us should visit one day, and while there, if we are lucky, move some really large rocks.

Thank you for reading and to quote the television star that started me on this journey over 25 years ago... "Live long and prosper".

Best Regards,

Michael Kohler
http://www.coralcastleexplained.com

Chronology of Edward Leedskalnin

1887 Edward Leedskalnin is born in Latvia 1913 Edward Leedskalnin, who liked to be called Ed, is jilted at the altar by his "Sweet Sixteen" and in his grief leaves Latvia.

1918 - 1920 Ed arrives in Florida City, Florida, after traveling and working in Canada, California, and Texas. He has also at this point contracted tuberculosis.

1920 - 1936 Recovering from tuberculosis, Ed buys one acre of land for $12 in Florida City. He proceeds to create a 200 ton "rock garden" consisting of coral carvings that resemble furniture in a home, and symbolic creations of enormous size and height, some weighing almost 30 tons. He is said to have created this place for his "Sweet Sixteen"

1936 Ed publishes his booklet "A Book In Every Home"

1937 Ed decides to move from Florida City, Florida to a 12 acre plot of land in Homestead, Florida adjacent to Highway 1. He also begins to move his 200 ton rock garden to this new location.

1939 Ed completes his move from Florida City to Homestead. He also begins to add on an additional 900 tons of coral to what will become the Coral Castle

1940 Ed completes what we now call the Coral Castle, opening it up for business again to the public.

1945 Ed publishes his books on magnetism and creates what some believe to be a perpetual energy device that he describes in his writings. The remnant of this machine is still at the Coral Castle today.

1951 Edward Leedskalnin dies of stomach cancer at the age of 64

Sources

"Mr. Can't is Dead" by Orval M. Irwin "The Enigma of the Coral Castle" by Ray N. Stoner

"A Book in Every Home" by Edward Leedskalnin Coral Castle pamphlets

McClure, Rusty. Coral Castle. 2009 MS. Amazon.com, Homestead.

Resource Links

Chapter 1

Coral Castle – Offical Site
http://coralcastle.com

Chapter 2

Tuberculosis
http://en.wikipedia.org/wiki/Tuberculosis

Chapter 3

Coral Castle Museum
http://coralcastle.com

Oolite (coral)
http://en.wikipedia.org/wiki/Oolite

Chapter 4

Dixie Highway or U.S. Route 1
http://www.us-highways.com/dixiehwy.htm

Coral Castle site
http://coralcastle.com

Ed "singing to the stones"
http://www.amazingabilities.com/amaze10b.html

Chapter 6

Latvian Star
http://fcit.usf.edu/Florida/photos/recreate/tour/coral/coral3/coral3.htm

Chapter 8

Polaris (North Star)
http://en.wikipedia.org/wiki/Polaris

Cardinal directions
http://en.wikipedia.org/wiki/Cardinal_directions

Great Pyramid of Giza
http://www.pbs.org/wgbh/nova/pyramid/explore/gizahistory2.html

Coral Castle book by Rusty McClure
http://amzn.to/11UGvqn

Chapter 9

Taj Mahal
http://en.wikipedia.org/wiki/Taj_mahal

16 Steps
http://www.crystalinks.com/cctower.jpg

Metal Door
http://www.coralcastlecode.com/imagelib/sitebuilder/misc/show_image.html?linkedwidth=actual&linkpath=http://www.coralcastlecode.com/sitebuildercontent/sitebuilderpictures/sun162.jpg&target=tlx_new

Ed's Well
http://www.mysteriousworld.com/Content/Images/Journal/2003/Winter/Artifacts/Map/Well480.jpg

Earth Labeled with Number 21
http://www.coralcastlecode.com/imagelib/sitebuilder/misc/show_image.html?linkedwidth=actual&linkpath=http://www.coralcastlecode.com/sitebuildercontent/sitebuilderpictures/thrownoutorbitsaeast.jpg&target=tlx_new

Chapter 10

Trapezoid
http://en.wikipedia.org/wiki/Trapezoid

Patterns in Nature (original site, now gone)
http://ourworld.compuserve.com/homepages/dp5/pattern1.htm

Fibonacci in Nature (same premise in that Fibonacci = Phi)
http://jwilson.coe.uga.edu/emat6680/parveen/fib_nature.htm

Phi
http://en.wikipedia.org/wiki/Phi

Golden Ratio
http://en.wikipedia.org/wiki/Golden_ratio

Phi and Harmony in Nature
http://www.natures-word.com/sacred-geometry/phi-the-golden-proportion/phi-the-golden-proportion-in-nature

Video 1 on Phi in Nature (awesome doodling video)
http://www.youtube.com/watch?v=ahXIMUkSXX0

Video 2 on Phi in Nature
http://www.youtube.com/watch?v=_w19BTB5ino

Phi in mathematics
http://www.maths.surrey.ac.uk/hosted-sites/R.Knott/Fibonacci/phi.html

Chapter 11

Phi as the 21st letter of the Greek alphabet
http://en.wikipedia.org/wiki/Phi_(letter)

Phi as the Golden Mean
http://en.wikipedia.org/wiki/Golden_mean_(philosophy)

Phi as the Golden Ratio
http://en.wikipedia.org/wiki/Golden_ratio

Phi related to the Greeat Pyramid of Giza
http://tony5m17h.net/Gpyr.html

Phi related to the Royal Cubit
http://www.grahamhancock.com/phorum/read.php?f=1&i=275811&t=275811

Phi numerically calculated
http://vashti.net:44131/mceinc/golden.htm

Phi represented geometrically
http://en.wikipedia.org/wiki/Fibonacci_number

Phi is found in ancient architecture
http://www.goldennumber.net/architecture/

Chapter 12

Pythagoras called numbers the "ultimate reality"
http://en.wikipedia.org/wiki/Pythagoras

Hyperdimensional Physics
http://consciouslifenews.com/hyperdimensional-physics/1120831/

Chapter 13

Hyperdimensional Physics
http://www.halexandria.org/dward118.htm

Richard C. Hoagland
http://en.wikipedia.org/wiki/Richard_C._Hoagland

Enterprise Mission
http://www.enterprisemission.com

Coast To Coast AM
http://www.coasttocoastam.com

Tetrahedrons
http://en.wikipedia.org/wiki/Tetrahedron

2 Tetrahedrons in a Sphere
http://www.enterprisemission.com/images/hyper/27lines.jpg

Geometric Proof of Tetrahedrons, Spheres and Phi
http://www.maths.surrey.ac.uk/hosted-sites/R.Knott/Fibonacci/phi2DGeomTrig.html

Image of Tetrahedral Geometric proof
http://www.maths.surrey.ac.uk/hosted-sites/R.Knott/Fibonacci/equilPhi.gif

Free Energy
http://en.wikipedia.org/wiki/Free_energy

Zero Point Energy
http://en.wikipedia.org/wiki/Zero_point_energy

Chi or Qi
http://en.wikipedia.org/wiki/Qi

Phi as the 21st letter of the Greek alphabet
http://en.wikipedia.org/wiki/Phi_(letter)

Chapter 14

Hans Jenny
http://en.wikipedia.org/wiki/Hans_Jenny_(cymatics)

Ernst Chladni
http://en.wikipedia.org/wiki/Ernst_Chladni

Cymatics
http://en.wikipedia.org/wiki/Cymatics

Sound affects matter geometrically
http://www.world-mysteries.com/sci_cymatics.htm

Aesthetic Calming Effect and Phi
http://www.maths.surrey.ac.uk/hosted-sites/R.Knott/Fibonacci/fibInArt.html

Mandalas and Labyrinths
http://www.labyrinth-enterprises.com/healing.html

Feng Shui
http://en.wikipedia.org/wiki/Feng_Shui

The Enigma of the Coral Castle
http://www.bibliotecapleyades.net/ciencia/ciencia_modernmegalithus02a.htm

Chapter 15

The Enigma of the Coral Castle
http://www.bibliotecapleyades.net/ciencia/ciencia_modernmegaliths us02a.htm

Stonehenge and Underground Water
http://www.journeyswithsoul.com/articles.php?id=19

Gret Pyramid of Giza and Underground Chambers
http://www.touregypt.net/featurestories/secretchambers4.htm

Teotihuacan
http://en.wikipedia.org/wiki/Teotihuacan

Hyperdimensional Energy
http://www.enterprisemission.com/hyper1.html

Etheric Energy
http://drlwilson.com/ARTICLES/ETHERIC%20ENERGY.HTM

Free Energy
http://en.wikipedia.org/wiki/Free_energy

Zero Point Energy
http://en.wikipedia.org/wiki/Zero-point_energy

Chi or Qi
http://en.wikipedia.org/wiki/Qi

Earth's energy grid
http://www.crystalinks.com/grid.html

Ley Line
http://en.wikipedia.org/wiki/Ley_line

Earth Energy
http://www.biogeometry.org/page34.html

Megalithic Stones

Coral Castle Explained   2006-2013 © All Rights Reserved

http://www.stonepages.com

Megalithic Structures
http://en.wikipedia.org/wiki/Megalith

Lunar Cycles
http://en.wikipedia.org/wiki/Lunar_phase

Lunar Phases
http://www.moonconnection.com/moon_phases.phtml

Ley Lines
http://www.ancient-wisdom.co.uk/leylines.htm

Ancient Sites
http://www.journeyswithsoul.com/ancient-sites.php

Lunar Cycles
http://www.moonconnection.com/moon_phases.phtml

Chapter 16

Vibrational Resonance
http://www.physicsclassroom.com/Class/sound/U11L4b.cfm

Dr. Masaru Emoto
http://en.wikipedia.org/wiki/Masaru_Emoto

Dr. Masaru Emoto's research
http://www.life-enthusiast.com/miraculous-messages-from-water-a-21.html

Chapter 17

Oolite
http://en.wikipedia.org/wiki/Oolite

Coral reef
http://en.wikipedia.org/wiki/Coral_reef
http://www.scienceclarified.com/landforms/Basins-to-Dunes/Coral-Reef.html

Calcite
http://en.wikipedia.org/wiki/Calcite

Trigonal Crystal system
http://en.wikipedia.org/wiki/Trigonal

Hexagonal Lattice System
http://en.wikipedia.org/wiki/Hexagonal_crystal_system

Quartz
http://en.wikipedia.org/wiki/Quartz

Many Uses Of Quartz
http://www.seidcrystals.com/aboutquartz.html

Chapter 18

Calcite
http://en.wikipedia.org/wiki/Calcite

Quartz
https://en.wikipedia.org/wiki/Quartz

magnetite in migrating birds
http://www.affs.org/html/biomagnetism.html

biogenetic material magnetite
http://www.biophysics.uwa.edu.au/magnetite.html

Pineal Gland
http://humanityhealing.net/2010/09/pineal-gland-the-transcendental-gateway/

Descartes and the Pineal Gland
http://plato.stanford.edu/entries/pineal-gland/

"The pinecone staff is a symbol of the solar God Osiris"
http://historical.benabraham.com/html/pine_cone_staff_-_solar_god_os.html

Pineal gland and Nature
http://www.conesandstones.com/historical-symbolism.html

The 3rd Eye
http://www.strayreality.com/Lanis_Strayreality/thirdtyepinealgland.htm

relationship to the Fibonacci sequence.
http://freedomfighterunite.webs.com/thepinealgland.htm

phi
http://www.goldennumber.net/fibonacci-series/

Pineal gland and the biomineralization of calcite
http://www.ncbi.nlm.nih.gov/pubmed/12224052

Thalamus
http://en.wikipedia.org/wiki/Thalamus

Chapter 19

Rupert Sheldrake
http://www.sheldrake.org/homepage.html

Morphic Field
http://en.wikipedia.org/wiki/Morphic_field#Morphic_field

Carl Jung
http://en.wikipedia.org/wiki/Carl_jung

Plato's theory of forms
http://en.wikipedia.org/wiki/Theory_of_Forms

Gregg Braden
http://www.greggbraden.com

The Divine Matrix
http://amzn.to/11GWRo2

Dr. Eric Pearl
http://www.thereconnection.com

Dr. Richard Bartlett
http://www.matrixenergetics.com

Chapter 20

Francis Crick
http://en.wikipedia.org/wiki/Francis_Crick

Albert Einstein's Theory of Relativity
http://library.thinkquest.org/28550/space.htm

Friedrich Kekule
http://www.bellaonline.com/articles/art19119.asp

Dr. Richard Bartlett
http://www.matrixenergetics.com

Machu Picchu
http://en.wikipedia.org/wiki/Machu_Picchu

Ed found nearly dead by realtor Rubin Moser
http://jayssouth.com/florida/castle/

Altered state of Consciousness
http://en.wikipedia.org/wiki/Altered_state_of_consciousness

Near Death Experience
http://en.wikipedia.org/wiki/Near_death_experience

Miami Circle
http://en.wikipedia.org/wiki/Miami_Circle

Chapter 21

Analemma
http://www.analemma.com/Pages/framesPage.html

Chapter 22

Quantum Physics
http://en.wikipedia.org/wiki/Quantum_physics

Quantum Entanglement
http://en.wikipedia.org/wiki/Quantum_entanglement

Morphic Fields
http://en.wikipedia.org/wiki/Morphic_field#Morphic_field

Chapter 23

PRISM Paranormal Investigations
http://www.doyouseedeadpeople.org

Chapter 24

Secret of the Universe Numbers - Revealed
http://www.youtube.com/watch?v=mER9eu3IVVI

Chapter 25

Stewart Swerdlow
http://www.expansions.com

Montauk project
http://en.wikipedia.org/wiki/Montauk_Project

Philadelphia Experiment
http://en.wikipedia.org/wiki/Philadelphia_Experiment

Electromagnetic lines
http://www.cancer.gov/cancertopics/factsheet/Risk/magnetic-fields

Nikoli Tesla
http://en.wikipedia.org/wiki/Nikoli_Tesla

David Sereda
http://davidsereda.blogspot.com

John Hutchinson
http://www.hutchisoneffect.ca

Counter Rotating Fields
http://www.esotericscience.com/Antigravity.aspx

Eugene Podkletnov
http://www.enterprisemission.com/anti-grav.htm

Chapter 26

Merkabah
http://somethingthatdescribesmeandmyarticles.blogspot.com/2013/04/merkaba-energy-fields-auras-ascension.html

Book of Ezekiel
http://en.wikipedia.org/wiki/Merkabah_mysticism

spirit Light Body
http://www.crystalinks.com/merkaba.html

Great Pyramid of Giza - Center of Earth's land mass
http://www.europa.com/~edge/pyramid.html

Hemi-Sync
http://www.hemi-sync.com/

Monroe Institute
http://www.monroeinstitute.org/

Binaural Beats
http://en.wikipedia.org/wiki/Binaural_beats

Chapter 27

Zero Point Energy
http://en.wikipedia.org/wiki/Zero-point_energy

Chi
http://en.wikipedia.org/wiki/Chi

Hyperdimensional Energy
http://www.halexandria.org/dward118.htm

Dean Radin
http://www.deanradin.com

Lynne McTaggart
http://www.lynnemctaggart.com

Made in the USA
Columbia, SC
27 April 2025